Revolution

and Counter-Revolution

Concepts in the Social Sciences

Series Editor: Frank Parkin

Published titles

Concepts in the Social Sciences

Revolution
and Counter-Revolution

Peter Calvert

Open University Press

Milton Keynes

Open University Press
Celtic Court
22 Ballmoor
Buckingham
MK18 1XW

First Published 1990

British Library Cataloguing in Publication Data

Calvert, Peter
 Revolution and counter – revolution. – (Concepts in the
 social sciences)
 1. Revolution. Theories
 I. Title.   II. Series
 303.6'4'01

 ISBN 0–335–15398–4
 ISBN 0–335–15397–6 (pbk)

Typeset by Scarborough Typesetting Services
Printed in Great Britain by J. W. Arrowsmith Ltd., Bristol

Contents

Preface

The principal purpose of this book is to re-examine the place of revolution in modern social theory, and to reassert the need for the systematic study of the social sciences. At a time when major changes are taking place in both the intellectual and the political climate, the one thing that is certain is that the world of the twenty-first century is not going to be as good as some of us hoped twenty years ago. However, with some luck, and the application of our intelligence, it may at least not be as bad as some of us now fear.

Observation

What is to be observed?

The more important a term is, the more probable it is that it will be incorrectly used. Most of us, for example, use the term 'weight' when we mean what the physicist would call 'mass' (or the physician 'obesity'). But in the social sciences the problem is particularly serious, since the words we use in everyday life have strong and well-established meanings of their own, and the attempts of social scientists to give them tightly defined meanings are seldom success-ful. So it is with the term 'revolution'.

In the 1940s there was no problem. There were no revolutions, or rather, there was only one Revolution, and the question was only how soon after the War it would come. Hardly anyone seems to have paid any attention to Katharine C. Chorley's (1943) excellent book on the subject, *Armies and the Art of Revolution*, perhaps because of the timing of its appearance, perhaps because it included some uncomfortable truths about how people use military force to gain their own ends and how those ends are not always those the masses want.

In the 1950s the Cold War dominated all thought and battle-lines were drawn. On one side, revolution was the hope of change; on the other, it was a fundamental threat to the values of the Free World. At the edges of the conflict, in the emerging Third World, insurgents struggling to free themselves from a colonial domination already on the retreat were caught up in the ideological matrix, and the rival alliances contended to make their struggles their own.

In the 1960s revolution was very fashionable. Everyone was making revolution, or rather, defining whatever they were doing at the time as revolution. Revolution was a warm, yeasty excitement which washed over quite sensible social scientists and left some of them spiritually transformed into bearded political activists. Defining revolution was counter-revolutionary, but writing about it was very fashionable, and a number of useful readers appeared as a result (Davies 1971, Kumar 1971, Mazlish, Kaledin and Ralston 1971).

In the 1990s revolution is no longer on the political agenda though it flourishes as a socio-technological metaphor. The Left has discovered the relative autonomy of the state and the class isolation of armed forces. America walks tall, rolling back the frontiers of communism, and the frontiers of communism roll back obedient to its command, as in Grenada. But in Afghanistan, as in Iran, do the beneficiaries not seem to be going to the Western civilization or the rational tradition of the Enlightenment (even the term 'Enlightenment' has been hijacked to describe something that looks uncomfortably like pompous obscurantism). Instead we wait to see which particular faction of Islamic fundamentalists is going to come out on top. We are going to need some clear ideas about what is going to happen next, as we may well not like it all that much. From the standpoint of the 1990s we can no longer be sure whether events in Iran and Afghanistan constitute a revolution or a counter-revolution. Clearly we are going to have to clarify what we mean by each of these terms.

Reading 2) a
Original Concepts

Origins of the term

'Revolution' in engineering is a unit of circular motion; in politics it refers to a sudden change of direction. The political usage originated in Italy in the late fifteenth century. *Rivoluzioni* were sudden changes in political matters, which occurred, it was thought, at times when the circling planets reached certain major conjunctions – for this was the age of astrology and *fortuna* was something of which anyone who would be a political leader had to take account. As late as 1662, Lord Clarendon was still using the word in English in this sense, to refer to the Restoration of King Charles II and the fall of the Commonwealth, whose rule he even attributed to the 'evil influence of a malignant star'. It was still a very broad term at the time of the so-called Glorious Revolution of 1688, the first sequence of events to be designated as a revolution by its contemporaries and adherents (Calvert 1970a). To this day the first definition given in the *Shorter Oxford English Dictionary* is 'forcible substitution by subjects of new ruler or polity for the old'.

In the course of the eighteenth century, however, as 1688 came to be seen not as an event in itself, but as the end and culmination of a process of political change that had begun at the time of the English Civil War, the term 'revolution' began to change its meaning. It retained, of course, its earlier, more general meaning. Fashionable reading for the informed in the early eighteenth century included the several works of the Abbé Vertot on the subject of the revolutions in Portugal, Spain and Ancient Rome, and among those who had copies in their libraries was Thomas Jefferson of Virginia. But slowly revolution began to change its meaning, as it came to be the term applied to a process of reordering government *after* political convulsions, of profound social change, of broadening participation in government and of progress towards a more humane society. Hence, when from the 1750s onwards the French began to talk of the need for a revolution in France, it was in this more specialized and more positive sense that they used the term. Contrary to traditional views, it was not the French Revolution that brought about this change nor even (given its remoteness) the American. When the Bastille fell in 1789 there was no doubt in observers' minds about what they were looking at. The Revolution had come at last, and, even before most of what we would now term the French Revolution had taken place at all, from across the Channel Edmund Burke, with the true instincts of a Conservative, had already denounced it.

It was the French Revolution, therefore, that was to set a permanent seal on the term, and to the previous usages was added another which today has almost displaced the others in social science usage. In the *Penguin Dictionary of Politics*, for example, the author, David Robertson (1986, pp. 290–1; emphasis added), is quite unequivocal in his strident advocacy of a very limited definition.

> A revolution, *properly so called*, is a violent and total change in a political system which not only vastly alters the distribution of power in the society, but results in major changes in the whole social structure. . . . in political science the primary meaning *must be* the deliberate, intentional, and probably violent overthrow of one ruling class by another which leads the mobilised masses against the existing system.

We can put Robertson's definitions to the test, for he gives us three examples: the French, Russian and Chinese Revolutions. The

Chinese fits the definition quite well. But the French fails the test: it was not intentional. The Russian also fails: it did not lead the mobilized masses against the system. Clearly this definition is too restrictive.

Giddens (1989) is more careful. He begins by saying what (for a sociologist) a revolution is not; a *coup d'état* which only replaces one set of leaders by another is not 'a revolution in sociological terms'. He then argues that a revolution must involve a mass social movement; lead to major processes of reform and change; and involve the threat or use of violence. Hence his definition is 'the seizure of state power through violent means by the leaders of a mass movement, when that power is subsequently used to initiate major processes of social reform' (Giddens 1989, pp. 604–5). However, this definition again produces anomalies. The Russian Revolution was not the product of a mass movement but of a faction. The movement was created after its leaders had seized power by means of a *coup d'état*. And though the Chinese Revolution of 1949 fits the definition very well, so, too, does Hitler's rise to power in Germany in 1933, since though he was first given authority and used state power to seize greater power by the systematic and deliberate use of violence, he was backed from the start by a mass movement. It should be noted, however, that there is no clear relationship between the seizure of power and the subsequent process of social change, and Giddens leaves open the question of just what we should call a *coup d'état* that is followed by widespread social change.

One thing that all observers will concede is that 'revolution' is a term properly applied to such major processes of social transformation and that such periods are uncommon. There is no agreement on how many there have been, but among those who use the term in this way there is a strong consensus that there have been very few of them. Examples that would be generally acknowledged are the English Revolution (still in Britain usually termed the Civil War); the American Revolution (still in Britain termed the American War of Independence); the French Revolution of 1789; the Mexican Revolution of 1910, the Russian Revolution of October 1917; the Chinese Revolution of 1949; and the Cuban Revolution of 1959. Perhaps a dozen more, ranging from the Chinese Revolution of 1912 to the Nicaraguan and Iranian Revolutions of 1979, would be widely – if not generally – accepted as legitimate examples of a major social revolution.

The mere fact that a difference exists between a general popular and a more restrictive professional use of a term is not, of course, a sufficient reason for using the popular term, nor is it necessarily a good one. But definitions there have to be; they are not an arid intellectual exercise but the very foundation of any serious thought (Sartori 1970). Definition is fundamental to any advance in understanding, and for definitions to be useful they have to be circumscribed. However, we do have to be careful in the social sciences that when we circumscribe a definition we do so for the sake of exactness and not for any other reason, and the problem with the restricted definition of the term 'revolution' is that it is not at all exact. Indeed it is so broad that it achieves the difficult feat of including so many phenomena in one definition that further analysis becomes almost impossible, and at the same time excluding so many examples that we can draw no useful conclusions from study of the few examples with which we are left.

Why, then, has revolution been seen as a major organizing concept? The reason is not hard to find. The French Revolution came when the Enlightenment had already paved the way for the general acceptance of the notion of reordering society according to a new and better model. But it came as a profound shock. In the words of Alexis de Tocqueville (1966, p. 35): 'What, to start with, had seemed to European monarchs and statesmen a mere passing phase, a not unusual symptom of a nation's growing pains, was now discovered to be something absolutely new, quite unlike any previous movement, and so widespread, extraordinary, and in-calculable as to baffle human understanding.' If the actual course of events was unexpected and even in some respects unwelcome, the practical demonstration in the heart of the leading state of Europe that a new order of things could be created by human will was to leave an indelible impression. Revolution was the path to the future. It came to be seen as a social process rather than as a political event, and one which, moreover, transcended existing political boundaries. Indeed, as fighting spread to Egypt, India, the Cape of Good Hope, the West Indies and South America, it appeared that revolution was a force with the strength to reshape not just the face of Europe but that of the whole world.

Small wonder, then, that Marx assumed – rather than argued or demonstrated – that the one instrument by which socialist society could be attained was through the new and wonderful force of revolution. For the rest of the nineteenth century would-be revolutionaries sought to learn how to control the levers of the locomotive of history. There must be a significance in the fact that they failed. There were many revolutions in nineteenth-century Europe, but none that are generally recognized as great social revolutions. There was unparalleled social change at the same time, but it was associated with evolutionary change and the emergence of a stable political order. Unification, consolidation and authority became the watchwords of a period in which governments gained in power over their subjects and, at the same time, the assumption of social progress was unchallenged. When they sprang to arms in 1914, the great European empires had partitioned five continents between them and were teaching the rest of the world to live like Europeans. The only two significant non-European powers, the United States and Japan, were well advanced along the road to industrialization and to empire.

Models of revolution

Extracting from reality the most significant set of interrelated properties of a phenomenon or an event is one of the basic tools of the social scientist. We call these sets of properties 'models'. They are not reality, of course. But because they form a simplification of reality they show up the significant variables more clearly and enable us to reason about them in a more effective fashion. The problem is that they also come in turn to shape our perception of reality in a particular way. We start to disregard evidence that does not match our preconceptions. We ignore conclusions because they do not fit easily into the selective reality which the model sets before us. Awareness of the limits of models is, therefore, an essential condition of using them effectively.

So it is with the French Revolution of 1789. Even after two hundred years the passions aroused by that remarkable sequence of events have not died down. The Revolution still serves as the type-example of the great social revolution, as, following George Sawyer Pettee (1938), more recent historians, sociologists and political scientists have termed it. The problem is to isolate just which of its properties are relevant in each context.

The *liberal* model of the French Revolution saw its outbreak as rooted in the failings in the existing social order. The representatives of the people, wanting redress of their grievances, called for and achieved representation through a National Assembly. Their

a)

Models

efforts to put things right, however, were frustrated by a combination of conservative forces: the king and the aristocracy, fearing for the loss of their privileges, the conservative powers of Europe, concerned for their own safety. The government, already bankrupt as the result of the mismanagement and inefficiency of the old regime, was unable to cope with the stresses upon it. The Revolution got out of control, as more and more radical leaders came to the fore, and a Reign of Terror ensued which might have been forestalled or averted had adequate measures been taken in good time. In the end, sated with blood, popular passions died down, Robespierre and his colleagues were overthrown, and the Revolution had devoured its own children. An era of relaxation, corruption and loose living followed, often called, after the French example, a Thermidorean reaction. This period in turn opened the way to the consolidation of a new and more technically efficient form of government, a military-led regime which in time became more and more like the old order.

Generalizing from this experience, later liberals placed the primary emphasis on constitutionality and representation. Once given the vote, the people themselves would secure redress of grievances, and orderly social transformation could take place. Mass uprisings, such as that in Russia in 1905, were a clear sign that the time for reform had come. So in Britain, when he heard the news that Tsar Nicholas II had yielded to the wishes of his ministers and dissolved the First Duma, Sir Henry Campbell-Bannerman announced in Parliament: '*Le Douma est mort. Vive le Douma!*' In the United States, with its own revolutionary history, there was an even clearer awareness of the way in which revolution itself could in the end lead to constitutional order. Thus President Taft greeted the fall of the monarchy in China in 1911 and its replacement by a constitutional republic as the latest and most dramatic demonstration of the virtues of constitutionalism, and Woodrow Wilson was in due course to seek to end generations of injustices in Europe by establishing the principle of national self-determination and the constitutional structure of the League of Nations that embodied its aspirations in a world that unhappily proved to be ready for neither.

Of course the liberal view did take account of the economic base of the grievances. Alexis de Tocqueville's study of the Revolution demonstrated how irrational the substructure of the French state had become by 1789 (Tocqueville 1966). Taxes were irrationally based and levied in different proportions in different provinces. Tax farming meant that the vast bulk of the taxes never reached the king, and exemption for the aristocracy meant that the weight of taxation fell almost exclusively on the peasantry. Tariff barriers between provinces, and between the provinces and the capital, arrested the free movement of trade, as did a complex currency and systems of weights and measures which differed from one area to another. The Revolution was a great act of rationalization which swept away the debris of centuries of administrative tinkering and established a new and more logical basis for economic activity. That reform over, early nineteenth-century economic liberals saw *laissez-faire* as the watchword and for Britain the repeal of the Corn Laws in 1846 enthroned free trade as a principle of government and ushered in an era of cheap food for a rapidly-growing population.

b)

Directly descended from the liberal model of revolution is the *functionalist* model, today exemplified by the work of Chalmers Johnson (1964, 1966) in the United States. Social systems have to perform certain functions in order to survive over time, among them that of system maintenance itself. Equilibrium in the system is maintained both by satisfying needs and repelling challenges to the regime. What were formerly termed 'grievances' are now seen collectively as dysfunction – aspects of the system that are not working properly. Multiple dysfunction, the failure of large parts of the system to work effectively leading to the alienation of many sectors of society at the same time, is the necessary condition for social revolution (Johnson 1964). The outbreak of revolution itself, however, follows when in this state of multiple dysfunction relatively small incidents serve as precipitants or accelerators to the revolutionary process. Multiple dysfunction plus accelerators equals revolution.

The *Marxist* view is in origin functionalist. Like Tocqueville, Marx and Engels took up the theme of economic rationalization, but came to rather different conclusions. For them, as for their contemporaries, the French Revolution was indeed an event of transcendental significance in world history and one which marked a major step in human progress. But its significance lay not in its being a move towards constitutionalism and the redress of grievances on a piecemeal basis, but a stage in the unfolding, underlying dialectical process of economic development. The real winners in the French Revolution had not been the republicans, the monarchists or the Bonapartists – indeed in Marx's lifetime the dispute had not yet been settled as to which of these three groups was to rule

France, and the world in which he died was dominated by empires even more powerful, to all appearances, than any that had gone before. The real winners were the bourgeoisie as a class, for classes, not individuals or parties, were the real actors in the historical process.

In the Marxist model of the French Revolution, therefore, the failure of the *ancien régime* lay in its economic inefficiency – the old feudal order had used up all its capacity to produce and was due for demolition. The calling of the States General enabled the bourgeoisie for the first time to become conscious of themselves as a class, and to act together to overthrow the old regime. The political changes that followed were largely irrelevant since at each stage they had a common aim: that of sweeping away the obstacles to economic development and liberating new productive forces. When the smoke of battle had cleared, the new order was fundamentally different from the old – the bourgeoisie, not the aristocracy, were in charge.

It was, however, not just his view of the French Revolution but also his deductions about what was to follow that distinguished Marx from his contemporaries. The bourgeoisie, he believed, owed their power to their ability to exploit the labour power of the proletariat. Bourgeoisie and proletariat were therefore locked together in a dialectical relationship, which meant that, just as the bourgeoisie had displaced the aristocracy when feudalism had ceased to provide an adequate base for production, so in turn the proletariat would overthrow the bourgeoisie when capitalism, which had brought such a remarkable transformation in the world, finally exhausted its productive capacity. The trade cycle, with its pattern of boom and slump, was itself evidence of the way in which capitalism regularly exceeded its productive limits, and the recurrent economic crises appeared to have immediate outcomes in political terms. The recession of 1847 was, Marx believed, the prelude to the revolutionary *annus mirabilis*, 1848 (Engels in Marx and Engels 1962, I, p. 120). Reviving confidence in trade heralded the return of the European reaction and the Bonapartist *coup d'état* of December 1851. Each new recession could be the sign that the ultimate crisis of capitalism was at hand. The Paris Commune, when for the first time representatives of the working class took their part in the provisional government of the capital city that more than any other epitomised the history of the European revolutionary tradition, strengthened this belief; as Engels wrote, in his introduction to Marx's account of the Commune, 'it was shown once more that in Paris none but a proletarian revolution is any longer possible' (Engels in Marx and Engels 1962, I, p. 473). In fact he was wrong: after 1876, when there was a brief peak in the vulnerability of governments to their own citizens, a long lull in revolutionary activity ensued, and *fin-de-siècle* Paris became a byword for bourgeois living. Yet the memory of the Commune lingered and became a myth, a metaphor for mass revolution spurred by urban insurrection, and when Yuri Gagarin became the first man to enter interplanetary space he took with him a small portion of the flag of the Communards as a symbol of what it meant to a later generation.

The Marxist model of revolution, therefore, places certain sequences of events at key points in the course of history. The assumption by the bourgeoisie of full political power came as a result of revolution – in England, through the Civil War and the defeat of the king, and in France through the creation of the National Assembly and its assumption of total political authority. It was assumed, rather than argued, that the ascent of the proletariat to power would occur in the same fashion, and that the social revolution of the future would occur first in the advanced industrialized countries, where the classes would be most completely polarized. However, towards the end of the nineteenth century it was already clear that this polarization was not in fact happening. Although wealth remained highly concentrated, social mobility was nevertheless possible and people of proletarian origin were being admitted to a share in the political process. In addition, governments had recognized the dangers, and in Germany Bismarck had introduced social welfare measures designed to mitigate the worst effects of the industrial order. Shortly before his death Marx, and subsequently Engels on more than one occasion stated that it was possible that the proletariat would gain power in these countries by constitutional means, without the need for an armed struggle. A further unforeseen factor was the rise and consolidation of nationalism. For Marx classes rather than nations were the major actors in history – his slogan was 'Proletarians of All Lands Unite!' (Marx and Engels 1962, I, pp. 21–65) and his vehicle for revolutionary action was the International Working Men's Association. Under the banner of internationalism, socialism had become a major European force by 1914. But when it came to the crunch, socialists in France and Germany voted for war, and though the traditional internationalist view born in the French Revolution and adapted by Marx was to survive, socialism itself was to be divided.

The Bolshevik Revolution of November 1917 instead was to give authority to a much more limited interpretation of Marx, the *Marxist-Leninist* model of revolution. This, though derived from the Marxist model and claiming in fact to be its only proper interpretation, had several distinctive elements. The social revolution was still seen as the product of the popular will; its legitimacy lay in the fact that it represented the wishes of the proletariat. A necessary precondition for the overthrow of the bourgeoisie remained that they should first have risen. But the Russian situation was so different from that which Marx had envisaged that a great deal had to be changed to fit the new circumstances.

First, there was the problem of the bourgeois revolution. Russia had not experienced one, unless it was the fall of the Tsar in March 1917, the so-called February Revolution. If this was the bourgeois revolution of Marxist theory, it meant a very considerable fore-shortening of the historical process, which, as will be recalled, for Marx was not just a question of the physical transfer of power but necessitated that the productive capacity of the bourgeois order should first be exhausted.

Second, there was the question of spontaneity. Marx and Engels, with the model of the French Revolution before them, had clearly seen revolution as a spontaneous mass rising. The revolutions of 1830 and 1848, and the Paris Commune, had all seen large masses in movement seeking political ends and economic transformation. Lenin argued, against the more traditional view of Rosa Luxemburg and others, that spontaneous action was not sufficient. The Bolshevik Revolution, he claimed, had been a true proletarian revolution, but it was the product of a party, organized to represent the wishes of the proletariat, and acting on their behalf (cf. Lenin 1968). Social revolutions in other European states would not just happen, they would have to be organized. It should be said that there was always some ambiguity in this claim, at least as long as there were people around who could still remember what had really happened in 1917. Sergei Eisenstein was afterwards to dramatize the taking of the Winter Palace as a mass invasion of tens of thousands of workers, whereas it was in fact the disciplined action of two hundred trained troops, and there were more casualties during the making of the film than there had been in the real event. But it is the myth, not the reality, that has been remembered.

Third, there was the question of what was to follow the revolution. Inevitably Marx had been vague on this subject. The 'dictatorship of the proletariat' which he envisaged as following the revolution is not as clear as later interpreters have thought and argued. In 1848 the term 'dictatorship' had not yet acquired the unrelievedly negative connotations of our own time – a dictator was still seen by many as an emergency office in the Roman mould, whereby all powers were granted to some person or persons acting in the interests of the state as a whole. Certainly Marx did not see it as the rule of one man but as the collective will of a class. Engels likened it to the government of the Paris Commune. The Russian equivalent of the commune was the soviet, or local council, and the cry of 'All power to the Soviets!' in Russia was taken up by the Bolsheviks during the heady days after the fall of the Tsar. Once in power, however, Lenin lost no time in subordinating the will of the Soviets to that of the Party, whose 'leading role' was to remain the principal distinguishing mark of Marxist-Leninist thought although not enshrined in the Soviet Constitution until 1977. It was the Party, therefore, that was the continuing beneficiary of the social revolution.

The revolution was to overthrow a class but it was also to result in the abolition of all classes and the establishment of a communist society. Yet realism showed that in the Soviet Union classes as such continued to exist, though Stalin argued that the elimination of the bourgeoisie left only two non-antagonistic classes, the workers and the workers on collective farms, and a stratum – the intelligentsia – which, though not regarded as a class, became in practice the ruling elite of Soviet society. It was left to a later observer, Milovan Djilas (1957), to argue that in taking on the mantle of power the Communist Party in Yugoslavia at least had not only taken on the appearance of a class, but had actually become a class. A ruling class, he argued, ruled because it controlled the means of production. Unlike earlier ruling classes, the Party did not technically own the means of production. But it did administer them as state property in the name of the proletariat, and by doing so acquired both the sense of consciousness and the concurrent privileges of being a class on its own account.

Djilas's claim came at a critical time, when the authority of the Soviet Communist Party over all other communist parties was being successfully challenged by Tito. For Lenin had not rejected the wider internationalist view of Marx altogether, but instead used it as an arm of state policy, and this tendency became entrenched under his successor, Stalin, who lacked his knowledge or understanding of the outside world and sought simply to enhance the power of the new Soviet government at home. Other European states showed little liking for, and practically no understanding of, the Soviet position, seeking to isolate it from world affairs by the creation of the so-called *cordon sanitaire* of small central European states. Attempts to break out of this isolation by appealing to the tradition of internationalism met with limited responses, and the creation of the so-called Popular Front governments of the late 1930s occurred too late and was accompanied by such suspicion on both sides that nothing lasting was achieved. Stalin's cynical alliance with Hitler could be explained away as an act of statecraft. It did not win any friends and the time gained by temporizing was wasted, but a lesson of sorts was learnt. After the Second World War, with the aid of the victorious Soviet forces in Eastern Europe, Stalin created a *cordon sanitaire* in reverse, to keep capitalism at bay and exclude its infection. Only in Yugoslavia had the Communist partisans under Tito established themselves independently of the Soviet Red Army, and consequently it was only there that Stalin's hegemony could be and was successfully challenged.

Apart from the Red Army, Stalin's most potent ally in the process of imposing revolution from above in Eastern Europe was the assumption of inevitability. It was widely believed that the revolution would occur, so when change came and the People's Democracies were established it was assumed to have been as the result of a revolution. It was also widely believed, in the West as well as the East, that once that revolution had taken place, it would be irreversible, in accordance with Marx's views on the trend of human history. 'Bourgeois' revolutions could be arrested, preempted or overturned, but socialist revolutions could not. So thoroughly entrenched was the resistance to a proper theoretical understanding of the causes of revolution that in the West it was not in fact until the late 1970s that this assumption of inevitability came to be questioned, and in 1981 Ronald Reagan's enthusiasm for 'rolling back the frontiers of communism' was still not taken very seriously. It was, of course, one thing for a policy to be theoretically feasible and another for it to be put into practice, and the lack of actual substance in the Reagan policy has in the event been disguised by the fact that for quite different reasons very substantial changes have been taking place both in the Soviet Union itself and in its relation with its allies in Eastern Europe. It is, therefore, a particular irony that some of those whom one might have expected to hail Reagan's success are in fact still warning gloomily that no real change has actually occurred – perhaps one has to look to Washington to find the last of the Marxist-Leninists!

Reagan himself also turned to good account the traditional liberal American view of revolution that sees it as the birthright of free peoples to take up arms to overthrow a tyrannical government. The American Declaration of Independence goes further:

> We hold these truths to be self-evident, that all men are created equal, that they are endowed by their Creator with certain inalienable Rights, that among these are Life, Liberty and the pursuit of Happiness. That to secure these rights, Governments are instituted among men, deriving their just powers from the consent of the governed. That whenever any Form of Government becomes destructive of these ends it is the Right of the People to alter or to abolish it, and to institute new government . . .

Reagan's description of the Nicaraguan Contras as 'the moral equivalent of the Founding Fathers' implies a view of revolution that is by no means as simple as it looks, however. On the surface, he is simply arguing that the Contras are the legitimate representatives of the Nicaraguan people exercising through the use of arms the rights claimed by Jefferson to alter or to abolish the existing form of government in their country. Unlike the American revolutionaries, though, the Contras were and are a force created, trained and funded by a foreign power. And the government they are seeking to overthrow is not a traditional monarchy or colonial regime, but a revolutionary government created by the Nicaraguan people themselves following a successful insurrection against a long-standing dynastic tyranny. (Had Jefferson been alive in the 1980s there is little doubt he would have been on the side of the Sandinistas.)

The problem for Reagan was that since Independence a conflict has grown up between the liberal American view of revolution as a legitimate means of changing governments, and the conservative view of revolution as a contagion spread by small groups of people from one corrupt state to another. He could not accept that the Sandinistas were a legitimate government, not because of the circumstances in which they came to power but because of the fear that they would act in a way contrary to US interests in the region by aligning themselves with the Soviet Union. But to argue that revolution is both a right and a wrong according to the definition of the groups involved is to be logically inconsistent (not that a touch of logical inconsistency has ever been a disqualification for high political office). Trapped by the Jeffersonian assumption that peoples have the right to do what they like, Reagan could only escape from this dilemma by arguing that the Sandinistas were not the legitimate representatives of the Nicaraguans because they did not constitute a free government. If it were they and not the Contras who were the 'foreign' element supported by a colonial-type power then it would be right to seek to overthrow them. Where the traditional liberal argument runs therefore, that the people have the right to choose whatever form of government they like, the *neo-liberal* position is that that form of government must, if it is to be acceptable, conform to certain formal criteria of freedom. In fact this argument fails for another reason – we no longer live in the 1770s, and today there are other considerations of international law and custom that we are required to take into account. But the neo-liberal model of revolution as something that is historically acceptable provided it fulfils certain formal criteria for acceptability is one which is widely held today and one which, in the form of the Brezhnev Doctrine, even had its reciprocal in the socialist states.

To sum up, therefore, there are certain attributes that are common to all models of revolution.

First, revolution is *sudden*. The gradual processes of political, social and economic change that go on all the time in all societies can and do result in major transformations, but they are not revolutions.

Second, revolution is *violent*. All political systems rely ultimately on the use of force (euphemistically termed 'physical coercion') and indeed it is the definition of a political system that it enjoys the monopoly of the legitimate use of physical coercion. But in revolutions coercion is not a last resort, it is the essential means by which change is to be secured. All revolutions that are universally recognized as such are associated with high levels of physical coercion.

Third, revolution is *political succession*. It requires *the replacement* of one ruling group by another. Revolution, therefore, belongs to a category of events the nature of which can only be ascertained *after* they have happened. Unsuccessful attempts to overthrow government, to gain control of the political system, to bring about far-reaching change; none of these is a revolution.

(There is in practice a small sub-category of events in which a ruler makes use of his capacity to use force to rid himself of constitutional or institutional restraints to the unfettered use of power. These can be regarded as revolutions, since, even if there is some continuity of personnel, the group as such is changed. An example is the most famous of the true *coups d'état*, the fall of the Second Republic in France in December 1851, or what Marx termed, again with conscious reference back to the type-example, the French Revolution of 1789, 'The Eighteenth Brumaire of Louis Bonaparte'.)

Fourth, revolution is *change*. If nothing changes then it is not revolution. There is little or no agreement as to either what sort of change must follow a revolution, or how much change is needed to qualify. The nature of change is highly charged politically, and therefore revolution is an essentially-contested concept (Gallie 1955–6) that is to say, one on which by definition no agreement is possible.

Where and why other concepts have been preferred

The essentially-contested nature of revolution has led some writers to abandon it in favour of other concepts that they find more meaningful or more pliable. The choice of such concepts is, of course, a perfectly valid exercise, and the relationships between them and the concept of revolution will naturally be determined by the purpose of the study.

Much of the history of the twentieth century has been conditioned by the identification of revolution with communism. The curious belief that only communists can make revolutions we certainly do not owe either to Marx or to Engels. Both were well aware that if their theories were true, the class best equipped to make revolution and most practised in doing so was the bourgeoisie. Instead the belief seems to have been one of the products of the Cold War following the emergence of the United States as a world superpower. The bipolar model of the world led Western policy-makers to internalize the Marxist assumptions, to assume that a real transformation of the world had taken place and that the only alternative to the existing order was indeed the long-predicted socialist revolution. By identifying all political change with revolution, and revolution with communism, they effectively succeeded in blocking necessary change and, in some cases – notably in Indo-China and in former Portuguese Africa – by identifying themselves with colonial oppression made the eventual triumph of Marxist regimes possible.

It was precisely the ideological presuppositions associated with the term 'revolution', on the other hand, that led a number of writers in the 1960s to try to develop in its place a new value-neutral term, 'internal war' (see Eckstein 1964), to refer to all forms of armed conflict within rather than between states. 'Internal war' is a useful and valid concept. The international community, which for legal reasons defines war as an activity practised by duly authorized agents of a recognized national government in uniform, has had in practice to come to terms with irregular wars of various kinds, subsumed under the generic notion of 'belligerency' which makes no judgement about the validity or otherwise of the aims sought or the means employed. Similarly, internal war adequately distinguishes armed conflicts lying within a single state's territorial boundaries. Such conflicts are fairly common. Often they do not appear to have any very clear beginning or end, and many of them do not appear to have any meaningful outcome in political terms. They certainly are not revolutions if governments do not fall and social change does not follow. From the point of view of a political scientist, therefore, 'internal war' eliminates what political significance the term 'revolution' has without any great gain in terms of understanding. Much the same can be said of the term 'turmoil' used by Gurr (1970) and favoured by other writers who have tried to develop predictive models. An alternative term which concentrates on the political while eliminating some of the military overtones is 'political instability'. This is a deceptively simple-sounding term which in practice turns out to raise difficult issues, and will be dealt with separately.

Revolution, then, is a complex term, embracing at least four aspects (Calvert 1967, 1970b). First, it refers to a *process* by which significant groups become disenchanted with an incumbent government or regime and move into opposition to it. Second, it designates an *event*, by which that government is overthrown by force or by the convincing threat of the use of force. Third, it describes the *programme* by which a successor government attempts to change some or all of the major postulates of the society for which it has assumed responsibility. Last, but not least, it refers to a political *myth*, a story which describes less how things were than what they ought ideally to have been. Though each is in some respects independent in terms of causes of the others, the common factor is the event. Only by the event is it possible to tell that a revolution has taken place.

Identifying the event in some revolutions seems simple enough. The fall of the Kerensky government in 1917, the flight of Batista in 1959 – these events were unique and decisive. But where is the event in the French Revolution? After all, Burke had correctly identified it as a revolution three years before Louis Capet was drawn through the streets of Paris on his last journey to the guillotine. The answer, however, is not complicated. The formation of the National Assembly was one turning point, the death of the king another. Both of these events, and others – the fall of Robespierre, Thermidor, the Eighteenth Brumaire – form part of a *sequence* which collectively we regard as the French Revolution. Each of these events opened the way for a regrouping of forces, and it was the cumulative effect of all these regroupings that determined the future course of social reform.

While Burke denounced the events of 1789 as a retrograde step in the development of France, Tom Paine and many others hailed them as a major step in human progress. So strongly held was the belief that a 'new order of the ages' had arrived that the *philosophe* and scientist Condorcet sketched out an outline of human progress as he lay in prison awaiting his execution. The fall of Robespierre and the Thermidorean reaction came too late to save him, but the belief in the inevitability of human progress survived, and for both advocates and opponents of revolution it became part of the accepted myth of revolution that once the forces of change had been unleashed, they would be unstoppable.

Such is not the case. Counter-revolution is not something different from and opposed to revolution. Counter-revolution is revolution. The use of force is something that is within reach of anyone who can command armed forces, and it is an unfortunate fact that such forces are much more often commanded by those who hate, resent and are resolutely opposed even to needful changes than by revolutionaries in the generally accepted sense of the word. Governments may fall to challenges from the right or from the left. The sequences of revolutionary events which yield progressive, reforming governments may equally well produce authoritarian dictatorships dedicated to pre-empting further change. The lesson of twentieth-century history is that they do so much more often than not. And the greatest problem of politics as the century nears its end is to restore belief in the possibility of real and effective constitutional change and to find some way of restraining the power of naked self-interest backed by the use of force.

Problems of studying revolutions

For some odd reason, those who study social phenomena are always supposed to be in favour of them. No one suggests that a geologist wants to see the world covered with volcanoes, and even those of us who feel sometimes that meteorologists are unduly enthusiastic about the prospect of bad weather would not go so far as to say that they are actually working to promote hurricanes. But the first problem anyone who tries to study revolution objectively encounters is suspicion about his or her motives. Of course those who study the phenomenon on behalf of governmental security organizations are not in fact objective, and this has led them to make some very serious mistakes.

By the nature of revolution, it is not a subject very amenable to study. Revolution is *sudden*. Time and again supposedly revolutionary situations have refused to materialize into actual revolutionary transformations, while suddenly, as if from nowhere, change overwhelms a state that had previously seemed stable. The *law of anticipated reaction* applies to revolution as to other social phenomena. The more it is expected, feared or hoped for, the less likely it is that all concerned will play the parts allocated to them in the scripts of their adversaries.

Revolution, too, is *secret*. Surprise is in itself a great strategic advantage either to the would-be revolutionary or to the government planning a pre-emptive strike. Revolution is not inevitably conspiratorial, but its does incorporate conspiratorial elements; it is not military in the formal sense, but all revolutions concern the loyalties of the armed forces. Evidence about the early, preparatory stages of revolution has to be pieced together after the event, often from individuals who have a very keen interest in perpetuating a specific view of it. There is, of course, no guarantee that the researcher will obtain an adequate coverage of all aspects of the process, despite its obvious importance.

Revolution is *complex*. Even the best-trained observer will see no more than a small part of the action. Those who report on modern revolutions will more often than not be professional journalists whose job it is to cover a wide variety of events in a number of countries. Such people are by definition very unlikely to have a specialist training in the study of revolution. At worst, coverage may be carried out by people whose training is completely inappropriate – an example was the coverage by the world's press of the events in Mexico in 1968, where the majority of those reporting were sports reporters assembled to cover the Olympic Games, who looked at a delicate political situation, saw it as a form of athletic contest between students and government and by presenting it as such helped create the disastrous outcome, the Tlatelolco massacre. Local reporters will be unlikely in such circumstances to act as a corrective, both because their local residence makes them vulnerable to government pressure and because their copy will in any case be sub-edited to fit the assumptions of their international colleagues.

The historian has the advantage here in having access, many years after, to the reports of another trained group of observers, professional diplomats. Since their sole duty is to inform their home governments their reports are confidential and they are of great value in helping to piece together an accurate picture of cause and event. The historical sociologist has the demanding task, however, of combining the tasks of the sociologist and of the historian – to use the skills of the historian in testing, evaluating and supplying the deficiencies of the evidence presented by the sources, and to use the skills of the sociologist to ask the questions about the evidence that extend and develop our overall understanding of the subject of revolution, an aspect of matters in which the historian may well have little interest. Contrary to the views expressed by historians and even some sociologists, historical sociology in this sense is a perfectly respectable branch of academic study (see *inter alia* Eisenstadt 1978, Hall 1985, Mann 1986, Mouzelis 1986 and Zeitlin 1988). Moreover, in the case of revolution the historical method is virtually the only approach open to us, and certainly the only one in which it is possible to give due weight to all aspects of the complex revolutionary process (see Zagorin 1982). For, as noted above, the essence of revolution to those who admire or fear it lies precisely in the fact that it stands at points of major transformation in world history. To ignore it on the grounds that a suitable method of study is not yet available, therefore, is to say that sociology is not yet ready to ask, let alone answer, the really fundamental questions of human social life.

Lastly, the size and scale of revolution can be such that it is *difficult to measure*. Social scientists rightly place a premium on accuracy of measurement and compatibility of data. What constitutes data, however, is not in this instance decided by the analyst but by the many observers, each of whom has a slightly different viewpoint. Each observer, therefore, not only records what was actually seen, but tries in two ways to develop the information available into a more complete pattern, either by making inferences from what is seen about what is not seen, or by seeking the opinions of others and adjusting the record of observation to make it fit more closely with the general consensus about what is going on. 'Cleaning' the data of such inferences is therefore a necessary discipline for the analyst.

The inferences themselves will be generally influenced by the prevailing model or models of revolution. In 1948, for example, rioting broke out in Bogotá in Colombia following the assassination of the radical Liberal leader, Jorge Eliécer Gaitán. His assassin was immediately lynched, so we do not know what his motives were, and they certainly were not known at the time. Yet within hours in the superheated atmosphere of suspicion that surrounded the incident, delegates to the meeting of the Organization of American States had concluded that the riots were the product of communist agitators, and the view that they were became instant orthodoxy and is still incorporated into many accounts of the period despite the fact that there is absolutely no evidence either for or against it. In such matters the analyst should perhaps set the example of refraining from unnecessary complexities of explanation.

Very few observers have much training in the accurate observation of mass events. Even in the case of peaceful demonstrations there is almost always a conspicuous divergence between the estimates of the numbers present given by the organizers ('about half a million') and by the police ('not more than five thousand'). The problem of measurement can, however, be exaggerated; the exact size is not necessarily as important as the duration of the demonstration, its target and the mood of those taking part. The question of what to measure and how to measure it is in this area as in others dictated by the purposes for which the information is required. If you ask 'how long is a piece of string?' you may quite properly get the answer that 'it is as short as it is long'.

To sum up, therefore, what we observe is conditioned by what we think we are observing, and what we measure is what we think is going to be useful to us. Many observers failed to realize what was going on in Iran in 1979 until it was too late – or rather, what they saw they did not correctly interpret as being a major social revolution designed to sweep away superficial evidence of Western-style modernization and to establish a theocratic state. They did so not because of any inherent inability to understand what they saw, but because of their assumptions about what the events they witnessed could mean. Prime among these assumptions were the twin beliefs that in the last quarter of the twentieth century religion was no longer a viable organizing ideology for social revolution and that economic modernization, in itself a good thing, would preclude the possibility of revolution of any kind. It is a considerable irony that a decade on, as we celebrate the 200th anniversary of the French Revolution, whose myth did so much to entrench both these assumptions in Western consciousness, the Iranian regime is still in power and, like some of the French revolutionaries before it, its leaders are trying to export its ideology to the rest of the world by threatening death and destruction to its opponents.

2

Interpretation

Interpreting revolution

What, then, is going on when we look at a revolution? The fundamental problem, for us as for others, is that revolution is a social process. Hence what it 'really' means is determined in terms not of some overall, abstract standard of measurement, but of the relevance of the process to the participant and to the observer. Some therefore argue that there 'really' is no such thing as revolution. Revolution is not a fact, or a set of facts, but a mental construct, a creation of the individual mind, and so has no real objective existence.

This argument takes us straight into the midst of the fundamental debate in the social sciences, which will be recognized by many as the so-called retreat from positivism. 'Positivism' is itself a value-laden term. Once a theory of human knowledge that placed society within the same orderly universe as the physical phenomena studied by the natural sciences, it has become a critical term applied (by its opponents, usually) to the view that society can and should be studied objectively by scientific criteria. Those designated as positivists (for few positivists, including most Marxists among whom it has become a term of abuse, accept the term as validly applied to them) have held that there is a distinction between facts, which can be objectively determined, and values, which are a matter of opinion. This view is now heavily under attack. The fact–value distinction, it is argued, is blurred because words not only can be but often are both descriptive and evaluative. Less convincingly, the conclusion is drawn that because the positivist separation between fact and value cannot be maintained in some cases it cannot be maintained in any and the enterprise itself must be rejected. To persist in such circumstances in trying to seek scientific explanations for human behaviour is to risk being branded as an 'empiricist' or even – to make the pejorative implications clear even to empiricists – as a 'naive empiricist'.

Both the attack on positivism and its Marxist analogue, the attack on empiricism, are attacks on the idea of a social science. Attacks on the social sciences are not new, of course. The concept of a social science is much disliked in conservative quarters and some have refused to accept the term. At Oxford University, for example, the social sciences are weakly termed Social Studies. Others succeeded in changing the name of the Social Sciences Research Council to the supposedly more relevant, business-orientated, Economic and Social Research Council. (Oxford, it should be remembered, was where Roger Bacon taught chemistry in the thirteenth century and was condemned to seventeen years' solitary confinement by the Church authorities for his impudence. The mind boggles at the thought of what the world would be like if Cambridge had done the same with Newton.)

Philosophical objections to the concept of a social science tend to be based on a very limited notion of what constitutes a science. They certainly do not take adequate account of the fact that a science may mean one thing to a philosopher and another to a scientist. The first problem of extending the scientific method to society, it is argued, is that society is made up not of inanimate matter or of sentient but non-rational beings, but of individuals capable of communicating and reasoning about their own condition. This leads to two inferences, neither of which is as securely founded as it looks.

The first inference is that because human beings are reasoning beings they can act irrationally and so their behaviour cannot ever be wholly predictable. This may very well be true, but again the conclusion drawn from it is not well founded. It is true that the 'hard' sciences such as physics (the very ideal-type of a hard science) deal in rigorously predictable events in the physical world. In theory, a physical experiment can be repeated endlessly and it will always give the same results. Certainly this is not true, and is never likely to be true, of the social sciences. Yet in recent years help in this respect has come from an unexpected quarter – sociology and political science may not be becoming harder, but physics seems to be becoming softer. At the sub-atomic level Heisenberg's Uncertainty Principle holds that no predictions about future behaviour can be made with certainty. Uncertainty is, it seems, built into the very structure of the universe. It does not matter in practice. At the level at which it is meaningful to us the traditional predictive statements still hold good: the switch is thrown, electric generators turn, the electric light shines, the coffee percolates.

The second inference is that theorizing about society cannot be value-neutral if society is itself going to be affected by the consequences of theorizing. This criticism, like Popper's (1957, pp. ix–x) proof of unpredictability, is based on a temporal fallacy. Value-neutrality can only be affected if the consequences of theorizing are capable of affecting the material to be analysed in such a way as to distort the process of analysis itself. Since by definition the consequences of theorizing cannot be known until afterwards, this cannot be the case. However, though theoretically possible, it is most improbable that future actors will in fact be fully aware of the existing body of theoretical knowledge.

A more substantial objection is that theorizing about society is not solely the province of specialists. We all theorize about society on the basis of our own observations and form hypotheses about how to behave – this is, indeed, the process that we term 'socialization'. How, then, do we form objective views about the world? The answer is simple: we ask others. The more people we ask the more our view of the world will approximate to value-neutrality. It is true that it will never reach it, but the approximation will serve, and the very fact that we seek to attain objectivity simply reinforces the central importance that it has in our scheme of understanding.

What has made the attack on the social sciences so effective, however, is not that the arguments of philosophers like Winch (1958) and MacIntyre (1983) carry much conviction in themselves. It is that meanwhile the concept of 'science' itself has come under attack, notably from Kuhn (1970), and his attack has been taken up enthusiastically by those who distrust the very notion of a social science and fear that if they allow it to develop, it will lead to the manipulation of some human beings by others. Scientists are now thought (albeit by non-scientists) not to do quite what they think they do. They do not and cannot establish a set of value-free ideas about the physical world based on observation, experiment and inference. First of all, their critics argue, what constitutes 'science' is itself socially determined. Scientists do not just study what they like since they work within a framework which determines what is thought socially useful and neither businessmen nor governments pay for experts to prove them wrong, or at least they do not do so intentionally. What the scientist chooses, or is encouraged to study is, therefore, value-laden.

Nor is his process of study as impartial or as reliable as he likes to think. Even where the experimental method is available for use, the scientist cannot prove a proposition right, he can only show that other propositions are wrong. Even the concepts of 'right' and 'wrong', however, are not his to determine. Kuhn argues that scientists work within a generally accepted framework of ideas about the world and the scientific enterprise which he terms a 'paradigm'. Scientists, therefore, work within the dominant paradigm of their day, practising what Kuhn calls 'normal science' (Kuhn 1970, p. 10), the repetition of standard procedures in a range of circumstances deemed socially useful but unlikely to challenge the dominant system of ideas. As new evidence accumulates which seems to challenge orthodoxy, however, they do not reject that orthodoxy; instead they try to fit their new evidence into the paradigm, even if it leads them into increasingly elaborate and improbable evasions. An example is the elaborate system of epicycles invented to explain why the observations of the actual movements of the heavenly bodies made by Tycho Brahe and Johannes Kepler were inconsistent with the Ptolemaic universe which put the Earth at the centre of all things. As in this case, when reconciliation ultimately breaks down, and only then, a new paradigm has to be accepted, and a 'paradigm shift' occurs. Perhaps scientists are therefore not so unlike politicians. They, too, find a dominant paradigm (e.g., the Cold War) impossible to reject until overwhelming evidence has accumulated through an increasingly long series of observations that reality does not fit the hypothesis (Shafer 1988).

This view is quite consistent with what we have already noted about the relationship of language to social reality. The existence of a paradigmatic model in the minds of researchers will necessarily mean that the vocabulary of the enterprise will be couched in terms of the paradigm. Early ideas about electricity, for example, were strongly conditioned by the notion that electricity was a 'fluid' which flowed along wires the way water does through pipes. This, as any electrical engineer will tell you, is not only not a helpful analogy, it is actively misleading.

Certainly we must accept that social reality includes language itself and with it the symbolic dimension. Language is structured in symbols and therefore consists of them. The language of politics is not a neutral medium, but a structure of ideas and meanings that channel thought in specific ways. But the point of politics is that it is about reconciling disputes and exercising power in the allocation of resources. Political argument is, therefore, not just about ascertaining who is right, but about who gets what, when and how. It may not be generally true, therefore, that language is the medium by which man conceals his thoughts, but it is certainly true of the language of politics. Many central terms in politics are essentially-contested concepts; that is to say they owe their importance to the fact that different individuals have very different interpretations of what they 'really' mean. Such disputes about their meaning are essential to their value as concepts and are, therefore, indeterminate. Where scientists seek agreement, therefore, politicians seek to conceal disagreement. The concept of 'revolution', most would agree, is itself an excellent example, since it will always mean different things to those who work for and those who work against it.

What value such concepts may have depends in practice, therefore, on ways in which individuals or social groups are attempting to structure thought. The fact that they are indeterminate or contested does not mean that no determinate or uncontested concepts can exist. The analogy with science holds good here. At one time there were no defined concepts in science and an entire specialized vocabulary had to be built up which attached very specific agreed meanings to the words used to describe physical processes. The history of the progress of science has been about establishing definitions for concepts which give them a fixed unchangeable meaning. It could be, therefore, that social scientists could fix concepts on the meaning of which we could all agree, and such a task has in fact been begun (though not, alas, finished) by the International Political Science Association. One example of such an artificial term, designed to be free from unwanted value-connotations, is 'internal war', as already noted.

The conflict over the 'meaning' of existing terms such as 'revolution' and 'counter-revolution' is not a debate that can be resolved (positivist view) but neither is it something that is wholly indeterminate and can never be resolved (post-empiricist view). The latter view in fact, far from demonstrating philosophical sophistication, would lead us away from the Age of the Enlightenment back to the arid wastes of theological disputation and the cultural stasis of the High Middle Ages. To accept it is to accept that faith, not reason, must be our guide. Yet, however unsatisfactory the basis of scientific knowledge to the philosophical critic, the fact is that it works. Man has got to the Moon by natural philosophy, through the practical application of a science that has left behind the rigid certainties of geometry and found that it is both adequate and practical to make a series of approximations.

Those who believe that science cannot exist without experiment may be reluctant to believe this, but much of astronomy and meteorology (for reasons of scale and distance) and medicine (for ethical reasons) is not accessible to the classic pattern of hypothesis-forming and experiment. Yet these are areas which have great intrinsic importance both to scientific understanding and (eventually) to our daily lives. If we were to abandon them on the ground that they were not 'hard' sciences we should be passing up the chance to ask fundamental questions about the Universe in which we live and condemning ourselves to deal only with matters of lesser importance. Precisely the same applies to the social sciences. The proper subject of mankind is man, and if we can only speak in probabilities, at least we can establish a basis on which such probabilities can be calculated with as much accuracy as may be practicable in the circumstances.

As a human construct, however, we must agree – and even assert – that society has its own dynamic, which is different from that of the natural world in the same way as electricity is different from water. Politics, for example, is, as we know, a way of determining who has authority to allocate scarce resources. But (like religion and sport) it is also a method of structuring time and giving meaning to life. The consequence of this structuring is that society is ordered and that within the social world the possibilities are by no means infinite. For the individual, understanding society means understanding a fairly limited repertoire of roles. It is certainly true that we cannot understand the social significance of a meal, for example, purely in terms of ingesting food. Meals can be expressions of family solidarity or conflict, of joy or grief. But the basic thing that we do at them most of the time is eat, and in doing so we adopt certain ways and mannerisms that are so thoroughly implanted in us that they become instinctive. So it is with politics. There are many things that can in theory be done, but if we wish to achieve our objectives we soon learn that many of them do not work. What complicates the issue, of course, is that these roles do not exist independently: the role of suppliant, for example, assumes the role of giver, and it is in the nature of society that one who assumes the one role will find the person he is dealing with similarly adopting the other. Each plays a part which is socially learnt in advance of the encounter. By this means the infinite (and infinitely dangerous) possibilities inherent in social encounter are regulated into safe predictable patterns, so that in practice the post-empiricist will find, for example, that when he asks for food he will be given something to eat and that when he asks the way he will not be told that, the concept of way being socially determined, it is meaningless for him to ask since any way he might be shown will be determined by the needs of the person directing him and not by his desire to get to any specific destination!

Politics is a form of conflict resolution between people playing well-defined roles and is, therefore, a drama. All political events, and above all revolutions, are dramatic performances acted out on the stage of society. In them symbolic strategies are quite consciously used for a number of purposes: to create solidarity, to attach meaning to procedures, to engender emotion, to incite others to action, even by ritualistic incantation to seek to inspire such vague attributes as public confidence or belief that the stock market is bound to rise (which it is not).

Revolution is widely regarded as the most dramatic of all social phenomena. The special significance of the French Revolution was that it placed France at the centre of the world stage at a time when following her defeat in the Seven Years War and inglorious performance in the American War of Independence, many in the rest of Europe were doubting her competence to face up to the challenge of modernization presented by the Enlightened Despots. It was infused by a conscious spirit of the neo-classical and led by men and women who acted out roles they had learnt from the myth and history of Ancient Rome. They intended it to be a turning point in world history, so in fact it became one: the events and processes of the Revolution may be the subject of legitimate dispute, but the myth is the more powerful for being insubstantial. The French Revolution gave France a powerful dictatorship and wasted the lives of her youth on the battlefields of the Napoleonic Wars. But it gave her glory, and as Anatole France makes a character say in *Penguin Island*, his satire on French history, 'glory never costs too much' (France 1930, p. 144).

The great revolutions continue to be stages for the great revolutionaries. Today Lenin and Mao Zedong lie embalmed in their mausolea while new currents of democratic thought have flowed through the streets and squares outside. Castro today is still playing the role of the young *comandante* of the Sierra Maestra, though he is now a bulky sixty-year-old in a baggy uniform which fits in none of the right places and he has had to give up the famous cigars with which he once made phallic gestures at the United States. Daniel Ortega, poet and president of Nicaragua, is grappling with the economic chaos which successive governments of the United States have visited upon his unfortunate country for seeking its own unaided road to democracy. Nasser is long since dead and the radical leader of the Portuguese Revolution has spent a long term in prison.

Meanwhile in Teheran Ayatollah Khomeini's death has been the signal for frenzied mourning; eight have been killed in the crush to get near the catafalque and hundreds injured. He has been hailed by the Western media as one who has done more to change the assumptions of the world than anyone this century. One radio reporter likened him in a single sentence to Hitler, Atatürk, Nasser and David Ben-Gurion. One could hardly have a more striking example of present-day Western cultural relativism, nor a more confused comparison. Atatürk, Nasser and Ben-Gurion were very different men and none of them was easy to deal with. But they were each true revolutionary leaders in that they believed in that idea of human progress which was perhaps not invented, but certainly gained impetus, as a result of the American and French Revolutions. And it is in the concept of progress that we find the extraordinary importance that the concept of revolution has had throughout the world in the last two hundred years.

On the eve of his death, fifty years after the American Revolution, Jefferson wrote what must be regarded as his final considered opinion on the revolution he had helped to lead. It makes clearer than a summary can what constitutes progress and what does not:

> May it be to the world, what I believe it will be (to some parts sooner, to others later, but finally to all), the signal of arousing men to burst the chains, under which monkish ignorance and superstition have persuaded them to bind themselves, and to assume the blessings and security of self-government. The form which we have substituted restores the free right to the unbounded exercise of freedom and opinion. All eyes are opened or opening to the rights of man. The general spread of the light of science has already laid open to every view the power of truth, that the mass of mankind has not been born

with saddles on their backs, nor a favoured few, booted and spurred,
ready to ride them legitimately, by the grace of God

(quoted in Butterfield 1959)

By these standards the Iranian Revolution of 1979 and the regime under which its people meekly surrendered their hard-won freedom to a religious despot marked a giant leap backwards for mankind and more particularly for womankind. Khomeini's despotism sought to destroy the foundations of international law and such limited principles of honest dealing as had been won in four centuries of warring between nations and replaced them by the shrill cries of Shi'a fundamentalism calling for an end to human progress (cf. Popper 1962, II, ch. 24). Happily we can be confident that, as Jefferson wisely forecast, such ideas will not prevail in the long run. In the meanwhile, however, for many, if the Iranian Revolution is indeed a true revolution, then the very concept has been hopelessly discredited.

In fact, in one sense the Iranian Revolution is a true revolution, and it is a measure of the extent to which the secularization of Western society has gone that so few of us realized in ádvance how powerful the forces of traditional religion could still be. In another sense it is a counter-revolution. And it is only within the framework presented by a concept of progress that the terms can be distinguished – there is no technical difference between a revolution and a counter-revolution; the process of disillusion with the existing state of affairs is similar, the mechanics of the seizure of power the same, only the programme to be followed thereafter is different. And yet it is not so different. The Levellers in England, for example, looked back to an ideal period in the past when England had been free of the Norman yoke. The disciples of Rousseau believed that man was naturally free, and that the structure of monarchy represented an aberration. The Bolsheviks moved the capital back to Moscow and turned their backs on Peter the Great's outlet to the Baltic. Time and again it seems that at moments of great social and political change people can only visualize the future in terms of an idealized past to which they must return. In this sense the Ayatollahs' Iran, with women safely cocooned in the *chador* and death for blasphemers and homosexuals, also represents a return to a never-never-land. For history suggests that when Islam was like this it was a weak sect in the desert; at the apogee of its power, when it was a world religion and people trembled at the sound of its armies, its caliphs lived in opulent decadence surrounded by concubines and eunuchs.

Analysis of revolution

As we have seen, many different views of any one revolution may be 'right', since they represent different views and not different realities. Whatever happened during the French Revolution, it is too big for any one mind to comprehend at any one time. The picture presented of it, therefore, is inevitably selective. However, it does not follow that the picture is analytical just because it is selective. By 'analysis' we mean something very specific: breaking down the whole pattern of events into smaller sections so that each can be examined in detail. Once this has been done, and general principles established governing the nature of behaviour at each stage of the process, we seek to recombine them in an overall model of reality. The second problem, therefore, is not that this is not done at all, but that, if done, it is done unconsciously, with the result that many unspoken or unwritten assumptions get built into the view of the overall process which can be distracting and, at worst, totally misleading. This might not matter so much except that in the case of revolution we are dealing with a phenomenon generally admitted to be of major social importance, but one whose significance as a phenomenon, to many writers, lies in its totality. Time and again, therefore, we find that writers on revolution are unwilling or unable to apply to their subject the same critical techniques that they would use with other social phenomena.

Systematic analysis of revolution as a phenomenon, therefore, has been a very recent development in social thought, and it is indeed an irony that the retreat from positivism should have held up progress on the exercise precisely at the point at which political risk analysts have been putting the knowledge already gained to work in the service of business and industry. Among earlier writers who sought to analyse in detail the component stages of individual revolutions were some of very great significance, including Alexis de Tocqueville (1966) on the French Revolution and Pitrim A. Sorokin (1925) on the Russian. As with later historians, they tended to focus on the causes and consequences of revolutions rather than the events which composed them, though, unlike many of them, they did try to draw general lessons about revolutions which could be relevant to other situations in other countries.

Once more it was comparison between the Russian Revolution and its earlier counterparts that was to stimulate the first comparative analysis of revolution. But here two assumptions speedily became apparent that have tended to colour all later writing. One was that revolution was – or ought to be – principally about ideas rather than deeds. A true revolution was one which dealt in the principal academic currency; other events that did not were hardly of the same significance. Hence historians of revolution tended to focus their, and our, attention on the great social revolutions to the exclusion of all other analogous phenomena. The French Revolution has generated shelves of books and – the ultimate in academic recognition – its own scholarly journal. Similar treatment has been meted out to the English Civil War, the American War of Independence and the Russian Revolution. By contrast, the study of the Mexican Revolution, in which ideas played a very different (and to some eyes much smaller) role has been left largely to area specialists, outside Mexico largely from the United States. Understanding what actually happened during the Cuban Revolution not only casts a sharp and rather unexpected light on the realities of power but also explains much of what followed after 1961. However, precisely for this reason, it remains an area of investigation which is highly contested, even though the facts themselves are quite recent, many key witnesses are still alive and the revolution itself was subjected to an unprecedented degree of scrutiny from the world's media. The Cubans propagate one myth, the United States another. And events in Vietnam, Iran, Nicaragua and Afghanistan similarly have currency in world political dialogue not for the sake of historical accuracy, still less the advance of social-scientific theory, but as slogans in a dialogue of the deaf.

In fact this very concentration of effort on the revolutions of the past in Britain, France, the United States and Russia, has generated another strange assumption: that these great social revolutions, each coinciding as they did with major changes in world outlook, were so special that they could not and should not be placed in the context of a general social theory, unless that theory was based on them. Pettee (1938, pp. xi–xii) puts this viewpoint concisely:

> I have not referred very much to the minor revolutions. From the great revolutions to such palace revolutions as Macbeth's murder of Duncan one could make an unbroken series of graded cases. But only the great ones give us any chance to estimate the importance of all the factors. The apparently latent factors in the social system may play an important but indeterminable part in any partial revolution. In various crises society may be disorganized with reference to any one of its axes of organization, as a depression or inflation may

disorganize the economic system. But only in a great revolution is it disorganized on all its axes. Therefore only in a great revolution does it come entirely apart, with all its internal forces revealed in the same light. Therefore it would seem that an adequate understanding of the partial revolutions can be arrived at only under the guidance of a theory of the total revolutions, because only the latter can give us a full picture of the complexity of forces which make an organized society what it is.

It should only be necessary to state this viewpoint to expose its essential falsity. After two centuries, and a further fifty years since Pettee wrote, it should at last be clear that the French Revolution is not going to happen again. It is in fact not the similarities but the differences between recent social revolutions that have been most significant, for time and again events have caught contemporary observers on the hop with no adequate theory to explain to them what they were watching. This is not surprising, for the method Pettee recommends is essentially one of reasoning from analogy about a complex phenomenon on the basis of a very limited universe of cases. An understanding of complex phenomena in every other sphere of human life has been arrived at by first developing an understanding of the simpler ones of which it is composed, not the other way round. The great revolutions form the greatest challenge to our ideas of social and political organization, but such challenges are in fact the daily stuff of social organization and social change. There is nothing that happened during the French Revolution that cannot be replicated from other historical examples outside the context of a great social revolution. We must, therefore, seek to treat revolution as a social phenomenon like any other.

Analytical treatments of revolution, therefore, have not attracted great interest outside the two separate, but related, specialist worlds of insurgency and counter-insurgency. Obviously people who want to make revolution want a textbook. Equally obviously, those who are paid to prevent revolutions need to know what they are preventing and to receive instructions on how to prevent it. For both, the purpose of revolution is to engineer a change of political power such that the new government can impose its blueprint of the future on society. The key, then, to the interpretation of revolution is the event itself.

It is a valid criticism of both revolutionaries and counter-insurgency writers that they tend to lay too much stress on the power of will. Obviously if revolutions were really grand, impersonal forces, there would be no point in trying either to make revolution or to prevent it. Both revolutionaries and counter-insurgency experts would then be best advised to heed Canute's practical lesson to his courtiers on the shore of Southampton Water, that even kings cannot command the tide. On the other hand, there would still be quite a lot of point in seeking a good theory of revolution. Knowing that the October 1987 hurricane was going to strike the south coast of England would not have prevented severe damage to property nor the loss of half a million trees, but it could have prevented some damage and it would certainly have meant that some people could have taken refuge in good time. Such commonplace and well-tried remedies as evacuation and storm cellars were highly effective in preventing casualties in the two Caribbean hurricanes of 1988.

We can begin, therefore, by identifying the three stages of revolution which Goodspeed (1962) terms 'preparation', 'action' and 'consolidation'. *Preparation* refers to that aspect of revolution which was earlier referred to as the *process* of revolution, the way in which significant groups or masses become detached from support for the incumbent government and/or regime and come to accept a forcible transfer of power to other hands. *Action* refers to the *event* itself, when the government falls as the result of the use of force or the convincing threat of the use of force and a new regime takes over. *Consolidation* refers to that stage following the change of power when a new government secures its own position and initiates a *programme* designed to change the social order. These stages are analytically relevant regardless of the amount of planning that went into the revolution in the first place. They are as much applicable to the French Revolution as they are to a military coup in Haiti. The difference comes not in the sequence of stages but in the nature of the social programme carried out by the successor government or governments. Such revolutionary programmes are the product both of social forces and of the power of will; that is precisely why they are so unpredictable.

The social preconditions of revolution

The social preconditions of revolution are those circumstances that bring together (or allow the bringing together of) leader, followers, a cause and the material facilities by which they can use violence to achieve it. These factors are common to all revolutions and though explanations of revolutions in a purely historical context have little or no analytical value, the historical circumstances in which any individual movement emerges as Touraine (1977, 1981) argues do determine its course and efficacy. Other writers have combined these elements in different sorts of ways with the social circumstances that facilitate them. Neil Smelser (1962), for example, lists six: the *structural conduciveness* of society to protest or revolt; *structural strain* leading to specific demands for change; *generalized beliefs* which structure a widely-based response to this sense of strain along well-defined lines; *precipitating factors* which touch off action; the existence of *co-ordinated action* (i.e. organization) to direct and support the movement; and the limited ability of mechanisms of *social control* to prevent the movement having a successful outcome. In distinguishing these preconditions, however, we will find it more helpful to discuss separately the social, institutional and personal factors that lead people to take up arms.

Social conditions

The likelihood of revolution should vary with the social predisposition to use force, but here the evidence is confused (Calvert 1984, pp. 64–78). Of those countries reporting very high homicide rates, Mexico and Colombia are stable democratic (or quasi-democratic) states where violent attempts to overthrow governments have not been successful for many years. Nicaragua has recently undergone a major social revolution and its continuing violence is the product of armed counter-revolutionary forces supplied from outside. The United States has a very high homicide rate by European standards, but socially is stable and conservative, though it was much less so in the nineteenth century, when it underwent a major civil war. Turmoil, or the prevalence of domestic group violence, may be associated with political and social change, but it sometimes comes *after* the event or when the impulse to change is frustrated in some way, rather than as a prelude to change or as part of the process of change itself.

Lack of confidence in or support for the prevailing government or social order again would appear to be a necessary social precondition for change. However, again the position is not as simple as it seems at first sight. As Gamson (1975) points out, the question of how many people support change is meaningless unless we know also how many people, and what sort of people, support the incumbent government. The balance between government and opposition is what will determine the outcome of armed conflict, not the numbers engaged on one side or another, and in the dynamic situation presented by a revolutionary incident the balance of forces can change extremely rapidly.

Class analysis was originally developed in the hope that it would yield definitive information about the outcome of a prospective social revolution. Discussion about the nature and meaning of class remains a staple of sociology, but modern views of class have now moved far away from the simple positivist model of Marx and his immediate followers. Class, too, is an essentially-contested concept. Perhaps more importantly, the very nature of the concept means that it cannot, as Marx hoped, be applied to each and every society; empirically-based concepts of class have indeed been developed, but they prove to have meaning only within the social systems for which they have been devised (Calvert 1982). However, writers of all persuasions continue to interpret revolutions in terms of class forces and no doubt they will continue to do so for a long time to come.

It must be said, however, that the emphasis many writers have recently placed on 'the centrality of peasants in modern revolutions' (Skocpol 1982, cf. Migdal 1974) seems particularly inappropriate from the viewpoint of 1990, and one of the mysteries of the last two decades is why peasant movements should have gained such popularity among revolutionary intellectuals, precisely at the moment when, because of changing farming methods and the drift from the land, their importance was rapidly declining. Even when peasants were common, and their unrest feared by governments, peasants seldom played a significant role in politics. Needing as they did to stay on their land to work it, they could be drawn to fight only on their home territory in its defence, or, very rarely, when the defence of their way of life left them with no alternative but to take up arms or die, as part of a larger insurrection. In this way, paradoxically, an essentially conservative social group comes to be associated with the most extreme radicalism, but it is the radicalism of desperation rather than of commitment. As the anthropologist Eric R. Wolf (1970, p. 301) put it:

> There is no evidence for the view that if it were not for 'outside agitators,' the peasant would be at rest. On the contrary, the peasants rise to redress wrong; but the inequities against which they rebel are but, in turn, parochial manifestations of great social dislocations. Thus

rebellion issues easily into revolution, massive movements to transform the social structure as a whole. The battlefield becomes society itself, and when the war is over, society will have changed and the peasantry with it.

Wolf's view was that this was both tragic and full of hope. For him the peasantry of the six countries he discusses – Mexico, Russia, China, Vietnam, Algeria and Cuba – were the vanguard of a better age denied only by 'the Holy Alliance of those who – with superior technology and superior organization – would bury that hope under an avalanche of power', that is, the United States. But his enthusiasm was premature, as was Che Guevara's (1967, p. 2) prediction: 'In underdeveloped America the countryside is the basic area for armed fighting.' The peasantry have not been and are not today a force for revolution as opposed to insurrection. The peasantry were the footsoldiers of the Mexican Revolution, not its leaders, and since 1940 others have spoken in their name. The same is true of the other examples Wolf cites. Moreover, it is not the United States that controls the destinies of the farmers of these states today, but their own governments. And the enthusiasm of those governments of town-dwellers to subdue the countryside to their will by what in effect amounts to a policy of internal colonization is strikingly consistent and gives little ground to believe that there will be a peasantry in the future, let alone that it will control the political destinies of nations.

Marx, among other urban intellectuals, wrongly concluded that peasants were just plain stupid ('the idiocy of rural life' (Marx and Engels 1962, I, p. 38)). With the peasantry disqualified as a properly revolutionary force the way was open for the new urban working class to take the lead. But his belief that the urban workers formed the basis for the future proletarian revolution stemmed more from the logic of the dialectic than from any realistic appraisal of their military capabilities. In fact, with the spread of industrialization and the increasing size of factories, co-ordination between factory workers became harder, not easier. The main aim of workers, like that of the peasantry before them, was to improve their lot at work. But unlike the peasants, whose challenge to their feudal lords at least threatened very immediately the structures of local government and administration in the countryside, the worker was remote from power centres and did not gain access to them without leaving his place of work. Furthermore, as governments were swift to realize, the local concentration of workers in individual factories or mines made them very vulnerable to governments prepared to use force, since they could be surrounded and if necessary starved into submission. The use of just this strategy by the government of General Barrientos against the tin miners in Bolivia in 1965 was to be recognized by Régis Debray (1965) as fatal to the chances of a socialist revolution, but unfortunately for him his enthusiasm for Guevara was to lead him to disregard his own advice. He went to Bolivia to meet Guevara, and was arrested, tried and imprisoned.

The position of industrial workers in post-industrial society does not give much grounds for supposing that they will form a major force in future revolutions. As machine-minders to robots they will either have little role to play, or, as technicians, whose importance to revolutions was first noted by Trotsky, a small number of them will be capable of creating disruption out of all proportion to their numbers. Workers and technicians in the public utilities have lost their leverage as the result of a deliberate campaign by governments to deprive them of it by fragmenting the industries which they potentially control. Governmental dependence on public utilities is already much less than is generally realized, owing to the organization of advanced industrial societies for war (Laurie 1970).

A third group which have been led to see themselves as the favoured vehicle for revolution are students. Students, as the cadet members of the ruling elite, in any country have unusual opportunities to take part in political activity and the 1989 unrest in Beijing is but the latest example of the way in which they reflect more accurately than their elders any widespread dissatisfaction with the status quo. What they lack, on the other hand, is experience and maturity, and, sadly, the history of student movements in politics is one of spectacular rise and sudden fall.

Social movements may come into existence for many reasons, and that of promoting revolution is rarely among them, if only because the heroic task of engaging in a seizure of power followed by a radical transformation of society is something that most people do not take seriously. In the Aberle classification of social movements (Giddens 1989, p. 625), only transformative movements – that is, those seeking radical structural changes in society – may be expected to have revolution on their agenda. The evidence is that such movements, however, rarely succeed in their grand objectives, and that social revolutions arise rather from a coalition of reform elements into a movement initially of a reforming character which gradually takes on a revolutionary complexion. Such coalitions characteristically combine elements from two of Aberle's other categories: reformative movements, seeking specific changes in the existing order (e.g., constitutional reform movements), and redemptive movements, seeking to rescue others from corruption. The task of welding such coalitions into effective political movements requires an institutional structure which is in turn conditioned by the institutional nature of society and the nature of the state.

Institutional factors

Revolution is not just a social process, but a political act (or series of acts) concerned with the seizure, consolidation and future use of power. Central to the interpretation of revolution, therefore, is an understanding of the nature of the state, the community as organized for political purposes. The fact that changes in the state are as much a part of revolution as changes in society has been repeatedly forgotten and rediscovered since it was enunciated by Franz Borkenau (1937). Pierre Birnbaum (1988) has drawn the well-known distinction between the 'strong' state, which can withstand challenges, and the 'weak' state, which seems to have been the precursor of many (though not all) of the major social revolutions; in the case of Brazil, for example, it was to strengthen the state that the military seized power in 1964 and ruled for more than twenty years. The state, however, is composed of a complex set of interlocking structures which impose institutional constraints on social action. Hence the importance of institutions to the understanding of revolution.

The most important institution from all points of view is the government itself, which stands at the centre of the political process as the target of political demands. Its day-to-day survival depends on its ability to convert these demands into satisfactory outcomes and thus by utilizing the resources of support which it enjoys, to generate further support and increased resources. In any state the centrality of government ensures that if anything is, it should be well known and well studied. Hence government should be that part of the revolutionary equation which is clearly understood. However, in practice the institutional constraints of revolutionary action are often not well understood even by governments let alone the political opposition, for three reasons.

Governments are *complex*. Regardless of the social origin of their members and the social groups from which they draw their support, they have their own institutional dynamic. This has a positive side: the rule of one person is no longer a practical possibility in a reasonably developed modern state. But there is also a negative side: the fact that, as Allison (1971) has argued, traditional 'rational actor' models of decision-making are simply not satisfactory explanations of what goes on in governmental circles. Hence, if governmental action can be seen as rational at all (which in itself is a highly contestable proposition) it is only in a very special sense, as being the product of individual rational decisions the collective rationality of which is assumed rather than demonstrated. Modern decision-making theory does offer a number of alternatives to the traditional rational actor model, of which the most important can be grouped as the organizational process model and the governmental (bureaucratic) politics model. But in each, the complex interplay of forces, either as between departments or between individuals, does not guarantee that we can predict the outcome of any individual decision sequence with absolute certainty.

This is concealed in many cases because governments have *institutional solidarity*. The individuals of which they are composed have more in common with one another than they have with outsiders, even those with whom they were brought up or who share a common class situation. In its extreme form this leads to the psychological aberration which Janis (1972) has termed 'group-think', the tendency for a collective body to persist with badly judged or even catastrophic decisions because individual members of the group, being reassured by their sense of group solidarity, fail to register their well-founded objections to the proposed course of action. Such insights are no less applicable to the past than to the present; hence the traditional view of revolution, drawn as it is from the age of monarchies, is not yet irrelevant but needs modification.

Governments are *hierarchical*. They stand at the apex of a complex administrative structure, and they rely on their staff, their line management and their links with the regions and provinces to make their decisions effective. Public policy experts have learnt from recent experiences of major decisions that have gone wrong or simply failed to materialize to attach great importance to the follow-through of decision-making into the implementation stage. In its extreme form, the *Yes, Minister* phenomenon, the staff can for its own reasons wholly frustrate the decisions of government, so

that, for example, governments that have sought to make concessions to revolutionary groups have found that at best their
orders are not obeyed and at worst they have been overthrown by
their own armed forces. In assessing the likely reaction of government the investigator must, therefore, ask some searching questions to which the government itself will not be keen to supply
answers: Are orders carried out? What instruments are at their
disposal to ensure that they are? If their authority is challenged
can they successfully resort to the use of force?

Logically we would expect those most likely to be involved in
the use of force to change government or society to be those
trained in the use of force and so having least inhibition in its use.
One group above all others stands out in this respect, and that is
the armed forces. Indeed so great are their advantages in this
respect that, as Finer (1976) remarks, what needs explanation is
not that countries fall under the control of military governments,
but that there are any which do not. Statistics show that over a
long period by far the most common form of armed intervention in
politics has been the military coup. But most governments that
come to power by such means last for only a short time and often
succumb to a challenge of the same kind as that which brought
them to power in the first place. Hence Finer draws a distinction
between the *opportunity* to intervene and the *disposition* to
intervene – most armed forces have the former, only some at any
one time the latter.

This works both ways. As already mentioned, it was Katherine
Chorley (1943) who was the first detached and impartial observer
to lay stress on the role of the armed forces in revolution and who
paved the way for the many studies of the military in politics that
have appeared since the Second World War (see especially
Andriole and Hopper 1984, O'Kane 1987). She was critical of
revolutionaries of the past for their failure to take account of this
factor.

> Practical revolutionary leaders, with the exception perhaps of the
> Russians, seem to have attacked their problems *ad hoc* with little
> reference either to theory or to the experience of the past. In
> particular, beyond occasional references of socialist thinkers or of
> long-headed politicians, generally of the Right, whose job has
> forced them up against dealing with revolution in action, little
> serious attention has been given to an effort to make an historical
> analysis of armed insurrection in its relation to the character and

strengths of the defending force of the *status quo* government which
the insurrection is designed to overthrow.

(Chorley 1943, p. 11).

It was Chorley, therefore, who first clearly enunciated a principle
which, despite some reservations, has stood the test of time well
enough to be accepted as an essential warning to anyone contem-
plating making a revolution: 'governments of the *status quo* who are
in full control of their armed forces and are in a position to use them
to full effect have a decisive superiority which no rebel force can
hope to overcome'. Revolutions, therefore, might be expected to
take place in the last stages of an unsuccessful war. Otherwise the
greatest threat to a government's control of its armed forces comes
from fraternization between these forces and the civilian population
which they are held in reserve to overawe. Such fraternization was
particularly noteworthy in France during the Commune, and the
provisional government under the historian Thiers had a remedy for
it; to withdraw the military forces to barracks and hold them in
isolation while they were purged before being returned to the field.
In 1989 the Chinese government has adopted precisely the same
strategy – finding that the units committed to the occupation of
Beijing were fraternizing, they withdrew them and sent in fresh
troops drawn from many parts of the country (and hence speaking
strange dialects and held together only by institutional loyalties)
who had been isolated from the news media for a period of two
weeks in advance of the operation. In modern times the customary
isolation of military forces from the civilian community has been
reinforced by the use of special anti-riot uniforms and equipment
which successfully alienate them from civilians as well as offering
them a degree of protection when they are called upon to act in an
internal security role.

Soldiers owe their particular importance in revolution, therefore,
not to their social origins but to their institutional strength. Their
institution is designed to imprint institutional loyalties, and the very
nature of the recruitment, selection and training of the officer corps
ensures that they form a select group insulated from the normal
structure of class and analogous to a caste. They therefore can and
do act independently of the social groups from which as individuals
they spring.

It has been a traditional assumption of both Left and Right that
the armed forces are necessarily the armed wing of the ruling class.

Leaving aside the fascinating but increasingly tedious question of what exactly the ruling class does when it rules (Therborn 1980), we should note that studies of the armed forces themselves show no such clear-cut assumption can be relied on. In fact the nature of links between the officer corps and civilians is such that in many instances civilians draw the armed forces into their political machinations and that, in an extreme form – as, for example, in Brazil – the process may be so completely institutionalized that an aspiring politician will have his military support just as he will have his financial backers and his party workers – they are all part of the institutional context of Brazilian politics. In such a context traditional notions of military intervention in politics and military government are clearly ones which have to revised.

The military role in revolution, moreover, does not end with the seizure of power or the use of social control to consolidate the power and security of the revolutionary government. As Adelman (1985) has argued, one of the main distinguishing features of the great social revolutions has been the fact that they raised the capacity of the states concerned to wage costly wars. The same phenomenon has been witnessed most recently in Iran, which employed mass mobilization and 'human wave' tactics to fight the Iraqi offensives to a stalemate and ultimately to a successful conclusion. Revolutionary Nicaragua also has been able to withstand a degree of pressure which would have been generally considered irresistible before 1979. As Skocpol (1988) notes, some qualification of the thesis is needed. Geopolitical considerations meant that the capacity of the Mexican Revolution to mobilize masses in foreign war (the Revolution itself, however, was one of the most costly 'internal wars' in history) was never tested, and it may well be that in consequence post-1934 governments were more successful in carrying out their social objectives than would otherwise have been the case.

Isolation from social currents is not an option open to the police, who by virtue of their role must live among the people and are therefore open to social pressures from them. Isolation exists – any police wife will tell you that – but it is isolation within society rather than the physical separation of military life. The police, therefore, develop their own sense of institutional loyalties within a society which they see very much in terms of an established order which they have the duty to maintain. There is an interesting parallel with criminals in that both tend to share the same basic assumptions about the natural order of society. In Northern Ireland since the outbreak of the troubles in 1969 there has been some rise in what some call (not altogether ironically) 'good honest crime', but the surprising thing to an observer from outside is the very conventional nature of the society and its assumptions. Indeed, it is the extreme conservatism of the society that has made it possible to sustain such a long period of violence.

The more militarized the police the more they will approximate to military behaviour and become an effective repressive force. Housing them in 'barracks', arming them, giving them helmets and clubs, and encasing them in vehicles all help isolate them as well as making them more effective users of force. However, they are usually regarded very much as second-class citizens by the armed forces and treated as subordinate to them. Governments, therefore, often cannot rely on the police when things begin to get out of control. Hence, it has been one of the main achievements (if that is the right word) of post-revolutionary governments to set up a powerful centralized security apparatus, both to protect themselves against counter-revolution and to enforce their programme of reforms. Though there is, in fact, a striking continuity in personnel in this respect between pre-revolutionary and post-revolutionary organizations, the organizations themselves were more rigorously structured and their powers extended in a way that only a widespread shift in social standards would have made possible.

It is not the purpose here to go through all the major institutional groupings of society showing their individual relevance to revolutionary processes. Enough has been said to show that revolution is a matter not simply of the mobilization of latent interest groups but of an institutional structure within which that mobilization occurs.

Personal factors

The behaviour of individuals, particularly in leadership roles, is so important to the origins and development of revolutionary situations that it is particularly frustrating that research into the personal motivation of revolutionaries is still so limited.

Personal factors can be sub-divided into social and psychological factors. Much of the literature on revolution continues to reflect the traditional assumption that what motivates one individual must necessarily motivate all, an example being Pettee's (1938) notion of 'cramp' as something experienced in pre-revolutionary situations.

But even in the case of revolutionary leaders, careful examination of their careers suggests that their backgrounds and attainments were nothing much out of the ordinary; what was unusual about their lives was either the group to which they belonged or the situation in which they found themselves at certain critical junctures.

Interpreting the event

The formal seizure of power, as we have already noted, is an essential part of revolution. What actually happens is that one ruling group is deposed by the forcible action of another, opening the way for further political and social changes (Calvert 1970b, Brier and Calvert 1975 and Brier 1982).

What happens to the old guard is clear enough. They are deprived of their formal offices, titles and privileges, separated from the network of power, placed under arrest, exiled and on occasion executed. Whether or not they play a further role in events depends not just on themselves but on the will and actions of others. Unlike boxers, fallen politicians find it relatively easy to make a successful comeback.

What happens to those who assume power is conceptually much more difficult. Even granted that in the society in question the forcible assumption of office is a recognized procedure entitling one to exercise the prerogatives of that office, the actual exercise of power is a very different matter. One modern revolutionary who erroneously believed that power went with office was Abolhassan Bani-Sadr, who fulfilled his long-standing ambition to become the first President of Republican Iran only to discover that the sort of republic he had helped to create was one that only allowed presidents to preside.

Epigrammatic it may be, but Mao Zedong's apophthegm that 'Power grows out of the barrel of a gun' is fundamentally wrong. Force is not power, as the rich man discovered who tried to power his pleasure boat with a novel internal combustion engine fuelled by small tablets of dynamite! Force can be instantaneous or intermittent; power consists in the constant exercise of will in such a way as to generate an assurance that a command will be obeyed or a decision implemented. Power in the last analysis is backed by force in the way that a currency is backed by gold or securities, but its day-to-day exercise depends on credibility. A government that continually resorts to force does not enhance its credibility, again because to look at governments in isolation is to miss the point of the exercise altogether. A government is only strong or weak in relation to the opposition. An opposition that becomes sufficiently strong can, if it wishes, become the government. What remains problematic is precisely why in such situations some people strive to seize the power that is within their reach and others do not. Much obviously depends on what they want to do with it.

Whatever happens an incoming government must consolidate its position. The consolidation phase can be divided into two stages though the stages of consolidation normally overlap with one another and the division between them is not a chronological one. The first stage is the consolidation of the government itself, the immediate measures that have to be taken to defend it against the possibility of counter-attack. These are normally short-lived, though governments can, and frequently do, prolong their emergency 'powers' in order to increase their relative strength even after it is no longer likely to be successfully challenged. The second stage may begin at once, though if it occurs at all it is often delayed by weeks or months. This is the implementation of a programme of wider social change designed to restructure society in a way that fits the ideals of the new government and incidentally adds to its chances of survival.

Such changes will be designated 'reforms'. Though the distinctive meaning of the word 'reform' has by now been so far eroded that it frequently signifies in practice little more than 'change', the word is used here precisely because it does still retain some connotation of social progress. In this respect, at least, the concepts of revolution and evolution are interchangeable. If they have a difference, it is that reforms reached through evolutionary change are much less likely to be successfully reversed. As we have already seen, there is in fact no difference in terms of procedures between revolution and counter-revolution; hence when one has occurred, the way is open for similar procedures to be followed by other groups.

Is it, then, the case that revolutions are bound to end in Thermidor, with many if not all of their gains lost for ever? Must reaction follow revolution? The answer is one which will please neither revolutionaries nor reactionaries. Reaction need not necessarily follow revolution, or at least, not within the effective lifetime of anyone involved. It is much more likely to do so where the successor government becomes entangled in expensive and destructive foreign wars which erode its claim to legitimacy. But modernized states can maintain a very efficient apparatus of surveillance and repression, such as Napoleon's Minister of Police, Joseph Fouché, could only have dreamt of. On the other hand, they rarely need to do so, simply because their ordinary powers, compared with those of any non-governmental group, are so great. Instead their greatest threat comes from within, and especially from the armed forces. So the reason why reaction does not follow revolution is more often than not that it comes first, and in the 1990s the question that will have to be answered is whether revolution in the traditional sociological sense is likely to happen at all.

3

Theorizing

Thinking about revolution

Theorizing is a great deal more than either observing or interpreting. Interpretation merely provides an intelligible picture of a phenomenon; it does not necessarily require us to give a full and comprehensive explanation of what is going on. The aim of theory is to provide that explanation, and to do so within a context which enables us to predict for the future what consequences may be expected to follow what events.

Earlier thinking about revolution was inevitably limited in its aims and objectives. With the French Revolution serving as the dominant example, explanations of revolution in practice were *sui generis*, forming part of the tradition of *histoire raisonnée* established by the Enlightenment. Comparative historical method began to emerge only in the mid-nineteenth century, after its principles had been outlined in John Stuart Mill's *A System of Logic*. Its breadth was limited only by the number of examples and by the time available; its depth was, however, severely restricted by the limited range of information available from standard historical sources. Despite this, the comparative historical method remains a major influence on the theoretical interpretation of revolution to this day, and, as argued above, remains an essential tool for understanding it.

It was in the tradition of comparative history that Marx himself studied bourgeois revolutions. What has made Marx such an important influence on later generations, however, is not his methodology (see Popper 1962, II), but the extent to which he convinced his contemporaries and those who followed him that his understanding of current affairs was something greater than that of a journalist. When it came to theorizing, he proceeded, as do all theorists, by the path of analogy, in his case drawn primarily from the field of economics. A crisis in world trade has been followed by revolutionary disturbances? Good! At the next such crisis there will be more revolutionary disturbances! The rich have concentrated wealth in their hands? They must somehow control the political order that enables them to do so. The fundamental assumption that political events were inextricably linked with economic phenomena was supported by historical instances – it was not tested by them. The very vagueness of the propositions meant that they could not be refuted. Hence it is possible for one Marxist scholar (Skocpol 1979, p. 34) to write:

> Marxist theory works with less general, more historically grounded categories than the recent social-scientific theories, and it offers a more elegant and complete explanation of social revolutionary transformations as such (rather than, say, political violence in general). It is thus no accident that Marxism has been the social-scientific theory most consistently and fruitfully used by historians to elucidate various particular revolutions. Yet the interaction between Marxist theory and history is incomplete because historical cases have not been used to test and modify the explanations offered by the theory.

Skocpol is in fact unfair both to the later Marxists and to non-Marxist social scientists. What elegance Marx's theories hold lies in the fact that they cannot be disproved. Marx never satisfactorily defines what he means by the classes which are the principal agents of change in his theory. He does not give a rational explanation as to why either the proletariat should seek power through revolution, or why the bourgeoisie should behave in a fashion that would allow them to take power. Nor does he give any indication of the time-scale needed. Hence the theories as they stand cannot form an adequate basis for predicting revolutions. Furthermore, it is clear to all that very profound changes have occurred in modern society since Marx's death. Hence later Marxists have had to modify the theory in a number of ways, either by stipulating additional conditions which must be fulfilled before a revolution can take place, or by reassessing the central role accorded to the proletariat in the seizure of political power, or by accepting a degree of independence of the state from the economic structure of society, to account for the effectiveness of governmental repression. As Jon Elster, who is satisfied with none of these solutions and advocates nothing less than a complete reconstruction of Marxism from the ground up, puts it:

> We must conclude, therefore, that Marx's theory of the communist revolution assumes that workers, capitalists or governments of capitalist nations must behave irrationally. Since he did not provide any arguments for this assumption, this theory fails. The point is not that events could not conceivably develop according to one of these scenarios. Irrational behaviour can be an extremely powerful political force. Rather, the point is that Marx provided no rational grounds for thinking that events would develop as he hoped. His scenarios were, essentially, based on wishful thinking, not on social analysis.
>
> (quoted in Taylor 1988, p. 225)

Writing on revolution in the latter years of the nineteenth century was relatively rare. After 1871 the hegemony of the greater European powers was entrenched, Europe itself was at peace, and, even after the beginning of the new century, revolution in Iran, Mexico and China was seen as merely confirming the success of European institutions. It is not surprising, then, that the substantial revival of interest in the comparative history of revolutions should have become evident again only in the 1920s. History was scoured for evidence concerning the possible future course of the Russian Revolution. It was undoubtedly important; the question was whether it was really a wholly new phenomenon or whether in time it would possibly follow the course of its predecessors.

In 1938 Crane Brinton, American historian of the French Revolutionary period, published *The Anatomy of Revolution*, a comparative historical study of the English, American, French and Russian Revolutions. In it he drew parallels between the four periods studied in a way that strongly suggested that the Russian Revolution had in fact much in common with earlier social revolutions and might in due course be expected to enter the period he termed 'Thermidor', the winding-down of revolutionary fervour and consolidation after a period of corrupt experimentation of a new and more efficient state system. However, as a historian, Brinton was cautious in his generalizations and laid much stress on the many differences between his case studies; indeed he specifically warned other scholars not to take his model as definitive Brinton (1952, p. 3), a warning which many of them have ignored.

Since the Second World War the emergence of new states has been accompanied by the occurrence of new social revolutions, and as the number of cases available for study has expanded, various authors have sought to study them in the same traditional context, using much the same criteria. Thus Leiden and Schmitt (1968) basically repeated the work of Brinton, taking as their case studies four examples that had either not previously been studied in a comparative context or which had occurred too recently: Mexico, Turkey, Egypt and Cuba. In a theoretical introduction they did, however, recognize the work of social scientists in seeking to derive from such case studies some more general propositions which would be useful in application to other cases.

Even more clearly in the tradition of comparative history is John Dunn's *Modern Revolutions*, first published in 1972. This deals with no less than eight case studies (Russia, Mexico, China, Yugoslavia, Vietnam, Algeria, Turkey and Cuba). Though treated on the basis of secondary sources and hence on a rather high level of generality, this book is informative, and the introduction and conclusion do challenge many of the traditional generalizations about revolution in an interesting and provocative way. Sadly, Dunn is so much influenced by British philosophical pessimism about the possibilities of constructing a true social science that he does not go on to extend the theory of revolution very far. He does recognize that revolutions are made by small elites who consolidate power to push through their programmes. He also accepts and describes the variety of methods by which power has actually been achieved. But he does not link the achievement of power to the nature of the outcome, except in the sense that both are recognized to be authoritarian. Revolution, for Dunn (1972, p. 255), remains 'essentially a metaphor'. But in the light of what has been said earlier about social phenomena being understandable only with reference to their social meaning, it is highly unlikely, if revolution were only a metaphor, that we should be celebrating the 200th anniversary of the French Revolution so actively. If it is a metaphor, it is an especially powerful and compelling one, in the name of which armies mobilize and men go out to die. It is also something that has meaning for people throughout the world, not just for the French. In the introduction to the second edition of this work Dunn (1989) recognizes this continuing appeal. He also dismisses all attempts to construct social scientific theories of revolution as 'hopelessly forlorn' (Dunn 1989, p. xxv), but happily, as we have already seen, this judgement at least need not be taken very seriously.

It is ironic that the book which did more than any other in this period to consolidate the prevailing sociological view of revolution as a rare if important historical phenomenon, Barrington Moore's *Social Origins of Dictatorship and Democracy*, was not really concerned with the theory of revolution at all. Rather, as its sub-title, 'Lord and Peasant in the Making of the Modern World', makes clear, it was an exercise in historical sociology in the grand manner, concerned with the way in which pre-modern societies had evolved, and distinguished from its predecessors in its recognition of the importance of land-ownership and the role of the peasantry in the history of Russia as well as of China. Like other unifying works of its kind, such as those of Spengler (1923) and Toynbee (1946), the book was instantly acclaimed as 'distinguished' and 'important' and virtually overnight achieved the status of a great work. One of the reasons was that Moore, a Harvard sociologist who had studied classics, taken a degree in sociology and served in the Office of Strategic Studies during the Second World War, was writing about modernization in the mid-1960s when it seemed most relevant to the preoccupations of the United States. Another was what has been euphemistically termed his 'independence' of existing historical schools and current orthodoxies. Moore debunks. The British like to think of themselves as peace-loving, but Britain is not uniquely peaceful. Americans may be used to the idea that their society is fundamentally different from others – a democratic state, conceived in liberty and resting on the will of the people – but this is mere wishful thinking. Moore insists that violence and coercion have played as much of a role in the formation of Western democracies as in the making of communist states or the rise of fascism: the differences between them, he asserts, can be found in the different nature of their revolutionary experiences. It was this theme, right or wrong, that grabbed the attention of his contemporaries and makes Moore important to any discussion of the modern theory of revolution.

Moore's method is, however, still that of the comparative historian. He concentrates on a few instances, the first three of which are traditional: Britain (which he calls 'England' – a common error, but one which does not inspire confidence), France and the United States. He then examines, by way of contrast, Japan, China and India, which he admits freely he has studied not because of his specialist knowledge of them but of their evident importance. This is a perfectly good reason but one which raises another interesting question about the basis of his work. 'That comparative analysis is no substitute for detailed investigation of specific cases is obvious', he warns us (Moore 1969, p. xi). Yet oddly enough, given that he was working as a Senior Research Fellow in the Russian Centre at Harvard, he does not give us a study of the Soviet Union, despite its relevance to the conclusions he is going to draw.

From the range of cases Moore studies, he discerns 'three main historical routes from the preindustrial to the modern world' (Moore 1969, p. xii). These, which we may prefer to regard as 'ideal types', significantly link the Russian experience with the Chinese and so with the current thesis on the relationship of economic modernization to revolution.

The first of these routes Moore (1969, p. xii) terms, not without awareness of the effect of the phrase as a 'red flag' to non-Marxists, the 'bourgeois revolutions'. These are the great revolutions and civil wars by which English, French and American societies came to combine capitalism and liberal democracy. The term 'bourgeois' is used so much throughout Moore's work that it is important to realize that he uses it effectively without definition; when it first appears (Moore 1969, p. 15) it is specifically defined to mean 'townsmen', but that cannot be what he means when it reappears, as it does again and again. The second route was capitalist and reactionary. Industrialization proceeded under the joint leadership of a small section of the bourgeoisie and dissident elements of the still dominant landed class, culminating in Germany and Japan in fascism. The bourgeoisie had only a weak impulse towards revolution, and if their aspirations took a revolutionary form at all, the revolution was defeated. The third route was 'of course' towards communism, after the agrarian bureaucracies of Russia and China had succeeded in frustrating the impulse towards modernization, and a huge peasantry was mobilized by the strains of modernization into providing the basis for a revolution that destroyed the old order. The common factor to each of these routes is the degree of mobilization, not of the proletariat, as in Marxist theory, but of the bourgeoisie. India he singles out as a conspicuous exception. It has followed none of the three paths.

> In that country so far there has been neither a capitalist revolution from above or below, nor a peasant one leading to communism. Likewise the impulse towards modernization has been very weak. On the other hand, at least some of the historical prerequisites of Western democracy did put in an appearance. A parliamentary

regime has existed for some time that is considerably more than mere façade. Because the impulse towards modernization has been weakest in India, this case stands somewhat apart from any theoretical scheme that it seems possible to construct for the others. At the same time it serves as a salutary check upon such generalizations. It is especially useful in trying to understand peasant revolutions, since the degree of rural misery in India where there has been no peasant revolution is about the same as in China where rebellion and revolution have been decisive in both premodern and recent times.

(Moore 1969, p. xiii).

The peasantry were unimportant to the making of modern society in England for a very simple reason: they had ceased to exist. The reason why they had ceased to exist was that state power in the hands of the nobility had been used to advance the enclosure of the public lands. As the lands disappeared into the hands of the big land-owners, local government also passed into their hands, but the big land-owners were not urban, as in France, or rural, as in Germany, but a mixture of the two – rural capitalists who advanced modern scientific agriculture and incidentally became very rich. The urban bourgeoisie rose, but the landed classes did not fall; instead, by well-timed concessions they incorporated the new elements and managed a gradual transition towards a wider power base.

In France, by comparison, the destruction of the old order by revolution was a necessary condition for democracy, and if the Revolution had not disrupted the growing alliance between nobility and bourgeoisie (as it might not have done) the outcome would have been similar to that in Germany and Japan. The Revolution opened up the way for radicals to free themselves from bourgeois control with the aid of the urban masses of Paris, a process which in turn was brought to a halt when the peasantry, having forced the dismounting of the seigneurial system in the countryside, ended radical experiment by cutting off the supply of food to the capital. The way was opened for a transition to democracy, but one which was to take a long time to achieve.

Moore dismisses in a few sentences the traditional view of the American Revolution. For him it is questionable whether it was a revolution at all. 'The claim that America has had an anticolonial revolution may be good propaganda, but it is bad history and bad sociology', he declares (Moore 1969, pp. 112–13). Yet the transition to industrial society was certainly not achieved without violence – it is the American Civil War that 'cuts a bloody gash across the whole record' (Moore 1969, p. 113), and the era of Reconstruction – revolution from above – that is the true revolution for the United States. It transformed American society, yet it was not inevitable that it should do so, for there was no fundamental incompatibility between slavery and capitalist methods, though it was essential for the consolidation of democracy that the federal government should be taken out of the business of enforcing slavery.

Peasant radicalism, such as Moore sees as being responsible for both the Russian and Chinese Revolutions, he ascribes to the inability of the peasantry, in the absence of modernization, to adapt to the stresses of modern production, and the alienation of the peasantry from local land-owners by the growth of the power of the state. By themselves the peasantry cannot achieve a revolution; they have to have leaders from other classes, and even then the majority of peasant rebellions have failed. In Russia the peasants had clear aims that the small Russian bourgeoisie failed to realize or to satisfy: 'to get rid of the landlord, divide up the land, and of course stop the war' (Moore 1969, p. 481). Only the Bolsheviks, with no ties to the existing order of things were prepared to promise these things to gain power. By the time the peasants realized they had been tricked, it was too late.

The rise of fascism was made possible in both Germany and Japan by the separation of government and society. Leaders came to the fore who were able within a conservative framework to bring about the economic modernization of their societies. 'Reactionaries can always advance the plausible argument that modernizing leaders are making changes and concessions that will merely arouse the appetite of the lower classes and bring on a revolution' (Moore 1969, p. 441). But in Germany and Japan the conservative leadership were able to see that the costs of modernization were paid by the lower classes, while building up a considerable bureaucracy and repressive apparatus freed future rulers from the need to take account of opposition. (It was not that there were not men in England who sought to do the same thing; the difference was that there the state was weak and the power to repress inadequate.) Fascism was a mass movement that mobilized poorer members of the middle class and rural elements in antagonism to capitalism, glorified an idealized form of peasant life just at the point at which it was ceasing to be economically meaningful, and used the concepts of hierarchy and submission to authority to magnify the force of their repressive apparatus.

Moore's conclusions are pessimistic. Both Western liberalism and communism (especially Russian communism) he believes may already be past their zenith. 'As successful doctrines they have started to turn into ideologies that justify and conceal numerous forms of repression', he argues (Moore 1969, p. 508). Much that has happened since 1969 in both Britain and the United States has only served to confirm that this prediction is alarmingly accurate. The costs of going without a revolution are high, and gradualism may occur too slowly. But the costs of having a revolution are also high. Communism cannot escape responsibility for Stalinism – every government blames its repressive measures on the need to outwit and outgun its enemies, and on both sides of the Elbe powerful vested interests stand in the way of a truly free society. Thus at the last Moore has no very useful prescriptive recommendations to make. His work conformed to the widespread belief of his period that revolution was an essential vehicle of economic modernization. But the absence of a case study on the Russian experience is surely crucial. The thesis that the peasantry were of major significance to the Russian Revolution is only valid in the sense that they were the principal victims. Moreover, the emphasis on fascism as the outcome of a failure to have a revolution is misplaced. The German Revolution did happen – in the form of the rise of Hitler to power and his use of that power to carry out far-reaching changes in German society. Those structural changes still stand in the German Democratic Republic, while in Austria, as the support for of Kurt Waldheim has proved, and in Bavaria, as the advance of the Republicans in the 1989 European parliamentary elections shows, fascist sympathies still run high. What prevented the German Revolution from being recognized as a revolution was once again that essential, if at times rather touching, belief in human progress, inherited from the Enlightenment and the days of the French Revolution, which led so many European intellectuals to assume that revolutions would always be of the Left and not of the Right.

The latest exercise in comparative history as applied to social revolutions is the work of Theda Skocpol, *States and Social Revolutions*. Skocpol intends by a rigorous, comparative analysis of three revolutions, described as the French Revolution of 1787–1800, the

Russian Revolution of 1917–21 and the Chinese Revolution of
1911–49, to 'reorient our sense of what is characteristic of – and
problematic about – revolutions as they actually have occurred
historically', and so offer 'a frame of reference for analyzing
social-revolutionary transformations in modern world history'
(Skocpol 1979, p. xi).

> In their broad sweep from Old to New Regimes, the French,
> Russian, and Chinese Revolutions are treated as three comparable
> instances of a single, coherent social-revolutionary pattern. As a
> result, both the similarities and the individual features of these
> Revolutions are highlighted and explained in ways somewhat
> different from previous theoretical or historical discussions.
>
>   (Skocpol 1979, pp. xi–xii)

Like the other writers discussed above, however, Skocpol starts
by defining her subject of study in terms so restrictive that it is clear
we are not going to meet any real surprises. Social revolutions 'have
been rare but momentous occurrences in modern world history',
which have enabled a limited number of countries (France, Mexico,
Russia, China, Vietnam, Cuba) to transform 'state organizations,
class structures, and dominant ideologies' (Skocpol 1979, p. 3); in
short, they are 'a complex object of explanation, of which there are
relatively few historical instances' (Skocpol 1979, p. 5).

> Social revolutions are rapid, basic transformations of a society's state
> and class structures; and they are accompanied and in part carried
> through by class-based revolts from below. Social revolutions are set
> apart from other sorts of conflicts and transformative processes
> above all by the combination of two coincidences; the coincidence of
> societal structural change with class upheaval; and the coincidence of
> political with social transformation.
>
>   (Skocpol 1979, p. 4)

Having dismissed existing social-scientific explanations of revolution as inadequate (why?), Skocpol goes on to argue that social
revolutions should be analysed from a structural perspective, with
particular attention to developments at home and abroad that affect
the breakdown of pre-revolutionary state organization and the
emergence of new organizations. Like Wolf (1970) and Dunn
(1972), she argues, she is using the comparative historical method to
seek the 'generalizable logic' behind the instances she studies;
unlike them she seeks to study these historical instances in depth.
But where she differs from virtually all previous interpretations of

revolution is in dismissing any notion of conscious purpose. For Skocpol, it is not too much to say, revolutions are the random product of structuralist conditions, and voluntarism plays no part in determining their outcomes. What concerns her is that the assumption of purpose will lead to the view that 'the ultimate and sufficient condition for revolution is the withdrawal of consensual support and, conversely, that no regime could survive if the masses were consciously disgruntled' (Skocpol 1979, p. 16). Any such impression she dismisses as 'quite naive', using white South Africa as an example of a 'blatantly repressive and domestically illegitimate' regime. Hence social revolutions are simply the unplanned product of competing forces. Different groups enter the fray and the outcome is determined by which of them ultimately wins out. Neither individuals, nor groups, nor even classes act throughout revolutions with the logic and consistency which traditional views would demand.

The state, however, is not just an arena within which conflicts are fought out for the prize of legitimate authority. Even Marxists, Skocpol says, while recognizing that the state is in theory coercive, still seem to imagine it in practice as an arena. She holds what she regards as the original Marxist position regarding the autonomy of the state. For her the state is 'an autonomous structure – a structure with a logic and interests of its own not necessarily equivalent to, or fused with, the interests of the dominant class in society or the full set of member groups in the polity' (Skocpol 1979, p. 27). The relationship of the state to the ruling class is not just one of simple subservience. In fact, the logic of production means that state organizations must compete for resources 'to some extent' (Skocpol 1979, p. 30) with the dominant class or classes, and may well allocate them, once appropriated, in ways either unwelcome or in extreme cases even threatening to the dominant class. Skocpol, unlike other Marxist writers, therefore devotes a considerable amount of time in her analysis of outcomes to the challenge to the new state organization presented by class conflict and counter-revolutionary military power.

Unlike earlier 'comparative' studies, such as those of Brinton (1952) and Dunn (1972), Skocpol does not examine each of her case studies in turn and then sum up her findings. Instead, following this theoretical introduction, the first part of her book is a very detailed comparative treatment of the causes of social revolutions, as evidenced by her three case studies. This treatment is divided into two parts: old-regime states in crisis and agrarian structures and peasant insurrections. The second half of the study, dealing with outcomes, is focused on the process of state-building, but here separate sections are devoted to each of the cases in turn.

The Marxist concept of class relations and class conflict forms the basis of the analysis in each case. She emphasizes, however, that this concept can only become effective through the modification of political structures. All existing theories of revolution, she claims, are voluntarist; this modification, she argues, must be seen in structural and hence non-voluntarist terms. Secondly, revolution cannot be understood simply on the national level. International as well as national conjunctures have to be favourable for a major social revolution to occur. But international conjunctures alone are not a sufficient explanation, so there is no support here for Immanuel Wallerstein (1974a,b) and the world-system theorists. Thirdly, classes are not the sole actors, and states are not simply the agents of the dominant class. States are both potentially autonomous and coercive. In fact, following Ellen Kay Trimberger (1972, 1978), Skocpol's concept of the great social revolutions is one of 'revolutions from above' led by elites in the name of the masses. Though social revolutions arise from mass action in the pre-revolutionary situation, the programme of reform that follows them is seen as imposed by elites operating within not only the limitations of the domestic context but also the international conjunctures of the world economic system, in particular, the structures of the world economy and the changing range of models available for borrowing. These are important, not because they influence the people, but because they influence their rulers.

In the last analysis, however, Skocpol's work, though elaborate compared with its predecessors, is too rooted in the tradition of comparative history to develop a satisfactory general theory of revolution. As she says herself, 'it needs to be stressed that comparative historical analysis is no substitute for theory' (Skocpol 1979, p. 39). Skocpol, like many earlier writers, excludes true theorizing, as she fails to understand that the logic of her argument is restricted by the framework within which she chooses to work. Many of the points Skocpol makes are simply not a problem unless you happen to be a Marxist. At the same time some of the things she ignores or dismisses are not just wayward bourgeois mystifications but fundamental points about the nature of scientific thought and the nature of social science. When she dismisses the need for a substantial number of instances as a necessary base for logically compelling theory, she does not appear to see that this is not a whim of social scientists but a necessary consequence of the mathematical conditions for accurate statistical reasoning. It is for this reason that so many other social scientists have worked to accommodate the theory of revolution to the study of other phenomena, with some success.

Thus in his collection *Rationality and Revolution*, Michael Taylor (1988) challenges Skocpol's argument that revolution is irrational, and he and his colleagues, also arguing from a Marxist perspective, seek to demonstrate two things: that rational choice theory can be applied to revolutionary coalition-building; and that the resultant findings are consistent with the many observations made by historians. He himself argues that, at least in the limited sense of rationality which is the foundation for modern neo-classical microeconomic theory and is used by Mancur Olson (1965), peasants are quite rational only to engage in revolutionary action when there is a reasonable prospect of success, and that it is for this reason that 'successful social revolutions have so far occurred only prior and during the transition to industrial capitalism' (Taylor 1988, p. 81). He further argues that there is nothing in the other structural and situational factors postulated by Skocpol that is not consistent with an explanation at least partly intentional. As John E. Roemer convincingly argues, in the same collection (Taylor 1988, p. 244), even if people act in revolutionary situations out of conviction rather than from pure self-interest, the very fact that they hold such convictions may well show that 'for an ethic or morality to achieve visibility, it must be relatively efficient, though that is not the reason people adopt it'. Thus the revolutionary ('Lenin') will in practice find that unless he is committed to progressive redistribution of wealth he is not likely to be very successful, while the government ('Tsar') will find that it will pay it to penalize the poor more than the rich, if it wants to frustrate revolutionary aspirations. We have already seen how Jon Elster is similarly able to use rational-choice theory to explain the failure either of the proletariat or of the bourgeoisie to behave in the fashion expected by Marx in 1848.

Social-scientific theories

Theory in the social sciences is a term that is much more restrictive than Skocpol's comments on it would seem to suggest. As Ted Robert Gurr (1970, pp. 17–18) points out:

> The central scientific criterion for theory is that it be subject to empirical assessment. Four attributes of theory that facilitate its assessment are its falsifiability, definitional clarity, identification of relevant variables at various levels of analysis, and applicability to a large universe of events for analysis. The first two are necessary conditions for assessment, the others desirable. A fundamental limitation of most older theories and conceptions of revolution is the difficulty of deriving falsifiable hypotheses from them. Few if any were formulated with reference to applicable empirical methods. The fact that very few case or comparative studies make use of them is further evidence of their limited usefulness even for taxonomic or conceptual purposes.

All this may be true, and, as we shall see, to his credit Gurr has himself tried to live up to the recommendations he makes. The problem is to achieve a synthesis between the three principal areas in which explanation has been sought: the psychological, the sociological and the political. This does not in itself seem to be an unreasonable task.

Psychological explanations

At least since the French Revolution people have sought psychological explanations of why revolutionaries act as they do. The early explanations, inevitably, are not very satisfactory, dealing as they do in such unscientific notions as innate human wickedness. Furthermore, even after modern psychology had begun to emerge as a science, the study of collective action was bedevilled by the notion of the 'group mind', which the French psychologist Gustave Le Bon (1960) argued was responsible for the way in which crowds acted in revolutionary situations. Though still influenced by the 'group mind' hypothesis (which he renders as a 'herd instinct'), Trotter (1953), who made the first major advance in this field during the First World War, recognizes the underlying importance of individual instincts (or, as we should now say, 'drives'). Everett Dean Martin (1920) rejects the notion of a herd instinct; instead he attributes the apparently amoral behaviour of crowds to 'a mutual consent to do the forbidden thing'. In this he follows Charles A. Ellwood (1905), who had already noted how people in revolutionary situations, being deprived of their normal frame of reference, may be expected to act in strange and unusual ways. Hence under revolutionary conditions old institutions collapse and change can be rapid and far-reaching in a way that in normal conditions would be impossible.

All overarching psychological theories of revolution fail on one obvious criterion: they assume that in a revolutionary situation everyone acts in the same way, that there *is* a psychological cause of revolution. In fact undirected crowd action has played little role in revolutions since the French Revolution of 1789, and though no one would deny the importance of individual factors in determining the role played by individuals in revolutionary situations, except in the case of a handful of leaders we still really know very little about why they acted in the way that they did.

Since the 1920s, fortunately, psychology, always dominated by the study of individual subjects on a clinical basis, has fought shy of group explanations of this kind. Though Freud's early studies of political leadership are read today more for the light they shed on Freud and his preoccupations rather than for information on the nature of leadership, it was Freud who swept away the notion of a 'group mind' and focused attention on the interaction of the individual with others.

Modern psychological theories of revolution draw in the main on data originally collected for other purposes. Because of its obvious utility to the selection of candidates for the armed forces and business management, among other occupations, there has grown up an extensive literature on leadership. A landmark in the field was the publication of *The Authoritarian Personality* (Adorno *et al.* 1964), which led to reconsideration of the role of leaders in a number of situations, including revolutions. One direct derivative was a study by Wolfenstein (1967) called *The Revolutionary Personality*, based on the careers of Lenin, Trotsky and Gandhi, and there have been a number of studies of individual leaders.

However, there remain two other difficulties with psychological explanations of revolution. First of all, it is not possible to apply clinical methods to political leaders, and the retroactive assessment of the personalities of historical figures, although practised by Freud himself, runs considerable risks of becoming purely circular: the leader did this, therefore that must have happened to him in his childhood. It need hardly be said that such speculations need confirmation from some other source, preferably contemporary with the childhood experience (e.g., a school report, early letters of the subject, family or friends etc.), if they are to be taken seriously. Second, leadership is not something exercised in the abstract, and it is certainly not just a function of the individual. The consensus of modern psychologists is that leadership is a function of four different but related entities: the individual; the group; the situation; and the task. Hence, though explanations of revolution may begin with the role of the revolutionary leader or leaders, unless they take in the wider social context in which the act of leadership takes place the explanation will have little value.

This is well illustrated by the work of Ted Gurr. His key work, *Why Men Rebel* (1970), is a highly formal exercise founded on a psychological hypothesis but branching out into a synthesis of current received wisdom. It is highly relevant to the problem of revolution but does not deal with revolution as such except in the broader context of political violence. Its purpose is to promote an integrated theory of political violence. It is therefore the incidence of political violence that Gurr is trying to explain, not revolution, and in so far as revolution requires successful use of violence his findings have to be supplemented with other information about the way in which political violence is actually used.

The impulse towards the use of violence is found by Gurr in a social-psychological concept already familiar from the clinical context of group violence. This is the notion of *relative deprivation* (RD), the term used 'to denote the tension that develops from a discrepancy between the "ought" and the "is" of collective value satisfaction, and that disposes men to violence' (Gurr 1970, p. 23). Conflict is seen simply as a special case of political violence, in which another group competing for the same values becomes identified as the cause of the discrepancy between expectations and outcomes. But Gurr wishes to avoid the conflict theorists' distinction between rational and non-rational uses of violence. Instead he distinguishes between three conditions in which RD can arise: decremental deprivation, in which expectations remain constant and capabilities fall in relation to them; aspirational deprivation, in which expectations increase but capabilities remain static; and progressive deprivation, in which expectations increase but capabilities fall. All three have been associated with political violence, but of the three, the first, decremental deprivation, which some have associated particularly with the rise of Nazism, Gurr believes historically to have been the most common. The second, the 'revolution of rising expectations' is a relatively recent phenomenon; it owes its peculiar interest to being the one most closely related to the Marxian hypothesis that concentration of wealth in a few hands would form the underlying cause of the social revolution to come. The third is, however, the form most commonly associated with major social revolutions of the past; generalized form of Davies's (1962) 'J-curve' hypothesis that 'revolutions are most likely to occur when a prolonged period of objective economic and social development is followed by a short period of sharp reversal', which Davies claims was supported by the evidence of the French, Russian and Egyptian Revolutions, the rise of the Nazis to power and Dorr's Rebellion in Rhode Island in 1842.

Each of these situations, however, only gives rise to discontent, namely, 'an unstructured *potential* for collective violence'. Belief in the utility of political violence, and the nature of coercive control and institutional support commanded by the incumbent regime, Gurr regards as the 'final determinants in the causal sequence linking hostile motivation to the magnitude and forms of political violence' (Gurr 1970, p. 155). Finally, he sets out a number of formal models as a basis for future multivariate analysis; in these he shows how his variables might lead alternatively to turmoil, conspiracy or internal war.

When pressed to explain outcomes, therefore, Gurr moves away from the psychological toward the sociological; indeed, his formal models, counterposing factors acting on government and opposition, are in fact elaborated conflict models. In the process it is easy to lose sight of the underlying questions that have to be asked: how do we know what the values of individuals are and how far their expectations exceed their capabilities? Hence, though his work is very interesting, it is interesting rather for the number of questions it raises than for the answers it gives.

Sociological explanations

The most popular sociological explanations of revolution, Marxist and non-Marxist, are functionalist explanations. The stability of society depends on the social order continuing to fulfil the requirements of its citizens. If it fails to do so, the underlying consensus on the values of society, which enables government to function, is lost, and with the failure of consensus the way is open for a mass rejection of the existing order. Such explanations tend to treat the actual transfer of power as a small matter, recording rather than facilitating social changes that have already taken place, and in the case of at least one revolution, the American, they are of course quite right.

An example is one of the first of the sociological writers, Lyford P. Edwards (1970), who drew primarily on the experience of the French Revolution for generalizations about the course of revolution. For him, revolution was of social rather than political significance, and this led him to play down the elements of physical violence and transfer of power. 'The overthrow of the monarchy and feudal system in France was not caused by the French Revolution', he argued. 'The Revolution simply made evident the fact that the real power in France had passed into the hands of the middle class' (Edwards 1970, p. 16).

The reference to France is significant, for the process of revolution, for Edwards, begins with that very French phenomenon, the transfer of the allegiance of the intellectuals. The intellectuals withdrew their allegiance from the old order and turned towards the vision of a new society. The fall of the old order increased both optimism and physical mobility; crime fell as the revolution was hailed as a reintegration of society. Government passed to the radicals because they were dedicated and unified. In power they acted with the confidence born of faith, using their power ruthlessly and with striking success – the deaths of their victims were incidental to the creation of a new order. But this period involved such strain on human nature that in turn reaction brought a return to normality, and such a return, often under the same rulers as before, is, Edwards argues, characteristic of revolutions as a class of events.

Pettee (1938) introduced as an explanation of revolution the term 'social disequilibrium'. Employing the terminology of Parsonian sociology, he saw society as fundamentally stable, and equilibrium is that normal state of society to which it will tend to return after crises or disturbances. The analogy is often used of a pond, where shortage of water leads to a fall in the number of fish, but if the water rises the fish will again multiply. The problem of making use of this concept is obvious. Societies, unlike ponds, are constantly changing. If the equilibrium point is moving, how is it possible to determine when a society has become so disequilibrated that fundamental change is inevitable?

A more systematic view is that of Johnson (1964; 1966), to which Gurr relates his notion of progressive deprivation. In contrast to Gurr, Johnson does not seek to determine the psychological motivation, but focuses firmly on the social processes involved. Moreover, he takes the logic of his argument a stage further than some of his sociological predecessors, by recognizing that, to be understood, the great revolutions must be placed in a wider context, and that this context necessarily includes the possibility of other, lesser forms of action. 'The phenomenon of revolution must first be placed within and related to the social system in which it occurs, and it must be considered in the light of what is known about social change and political development.' This leads Johnson (1964, p. 2) to adopt as his provisional definition of revolution that of Sigmund Neumann (1949, pp. 333–4): 'a sweeping fundamental change in political organization, social structure, economic property control and the predominant myth of a social order, thus indicating a major break in the continuity of development'. Unlike Hannah Arendt (1963), who emphasizes that revolutions are not just changes, Johnson properly reminds us that this is what they are and that we should recognize the fact. Revolution is social change, the outcome of severe systemic disequilibrium in certain circumstances. Social dysfunction resulting from disequilibrium is a necessary cause of revolution, when confronted by another, elite intransigence. 'It takes two to make a revolution, and one of these two is always the status quo elite' (Johnson 1964, p. 6). The sufficient cause is any incident which serves as an 'accelerator of dysfunction', that is to say one of a number of 'occurrences that catalyze or throw into relief the already existent revolutionary level of dysfunctions' (Johnson 1964, p. 12). A modern Marxist might say that social revolutions are 'overdetermined'.

Johnson, like Chorley, attributes crucial significance to the role of the armed forces. Revolution, for him, implies armed insurrection; if change takes place without insurrection, there has been change but not revolution. The example he gives is that of the fall of the Tokugawa shogunate in Japan, though it is only fair to say that there was in fact an element of implied force in this and that many scholars do now refer to the Meiji Restoration as a revolution. There can be no doubt, however, that where a government is fully backed by the armed might of a well-trained and loyal army, then insurrection against it will not succeed. And since officers form part of the elite, and other ranks are effectively isolated from the society in which they live, this means that the armed forces have a high degree of autonomy in a revolutionary situation.

This leads to Johnson developing a six-fold typology of

revolution; jacquerie; millenarian rebellion; anarchistic rebellion; jacobin communist revolution; conspiratorial *coup d'état*; and militarized mass insurrection. Identifying these categories involves the use of four criteria: the targets of the activity; the nature of the revolutionaries; the goals of the revolution; and whether it is planned or develops spontaneously.

The *jacquerie* is a mass rebellion of peasants with the limited aim of redressing grievances. The *millenarian rebellion*, urban or rural, is a rising in the hope of a radical change in a world in which all will be made anew. *Anarchistic rebellions* are a reaction to modernization opposing governmental authority and seeking to return to an older order regarded with nostalgia. All three involve mass action and much spontaneity. In the other three categories, elites lead masses and plan action accordingly. *Jacobin communist revolutions* 'are the "great" revolutions' (Johnson 1964, p. 45), and the French Revolution is given as the classic example of this very small category. But, in fact, one example of a so-called great revolution falls in the fifth category, that of *conspiratorial coups d'état* (why conspiratorial? are not all *coups d'état* conspiratorial?), and one in the sixth, *militarized mass insurrection*, otherwise known to *cognoscenti* as 'guerrilla warfare'.

The weakness of this classification is obvious. There is no clear reason why these six categories *and no others* have been selected. Indeed many of the examples of the first three (jacquerie, millenarian rebellion, anarchistic rebellion) can hardly be regarded as revolutions at all, since they failed either to bring down governments or to change the social system. As a sociologist, Johnson defends the view that the distinction between rebellion and revolution is for some purposes unimportant; though when it comes to the strategies of revolution, there is all the difference in the world between failure and success. Benjamin Franklin put the revolutionaries' need for success most succinctly when he declared: 'We must hang together, for if we do not, assuredly we shall all hang separately.' However, Johnson (1964) deserves credit for recognizing that the logic which leads people to study the great revolutions in the first place means that they also have to study the lesser ones.

In his *Revolutionary Change*, Johnson (1966) modifies his position, re-emphasizing the importance of equilibrium and seeing its failure as the result of the structure of social values getting out of line with change in the sociopolitical environment. As change happens, he argues, a situation of 'power deflation' arises in which the ruling elite resort to increasing force to maintain their position, and if they fail to adjust to changing conditions of society, the basic preconditions for revolution are present. Johnson goes on to look for indicators of disequilibrium which might be used as the basis of an index of the propensity for revolution within a society. Suicide, crime and the military participation ratio are offered as possibilities, and recent work on what is now termed 'political risk' has identified others. As before, the final precipitant of revolution is an 'accelerator' of some kind, but accelerators, by their nature, are so unpredictable that they defy systematization.

The problem with all these explanations is that they do not explain very well why revolutions do happen, and they explain even less well why they do not happen. History is full of examples of states and societies that on these criteria should have been short-lived, yet have somehow managed to survive. For the nineteenth century the Austro-Hungarian Empire is a particularly striking example; from a sociological point of view it was a time bomb just waiting to explode. But it took a world war for that explosion actually to happen. The apparently more coherent, logically organized states carved out of it, on the other hand, offer proof of how far logic can fall short of tradition as a vehicle for political stability. Hungary, Yugoslavia and Czechoslovakia have each in very different ways been symbols to the post-1945 world of the failure of social engineering to reconcile a supposedly willing people with the well-intentioned plans of their ruling elite.

Gurr's (1970) model of political violence, discussed above, contains substantial consideration of the way in which masses become alienated from their rulers and resort to violence. In a similar vein, William L. Gamson (1975) has attempted to determine levels of support for and against government at key periods in revolutionary situations. With public opinion polls a fact of life in much of the world, and no longer only in the advanced democratic societies, there will obviously be data available for the future analyst of revolution which we can still only infer about the events of the historical past.

Political explanations

The analysis of revolution presented above in Chapter 2 is a view of revolution from the point of view of a political scientist, and falls into a group of political conflict theories of revolution of which perhaps the best known is that of the sociologist and historian, Charles Tilly of the University of Michigan.

Since what makes a revolution a revolution (as opposed to a disturbance, a rising, a rebellion or an insurrection) is the transfer of political power, political conflict theorists see political conflict as the basic cause of revolution. Tilly (1978, p. 193) defines the *sine qua non* of revolution thus: 'A revolutionary outcome is the displacement of one set of power holders by another.' I would term it a revolutionary event and hence prefer the definition used in my *A Study of Revolution* (Calvert 1970b, p. 5) of 'a change of government (transition) at a clearly defined point in time by the use of armed force, or the credible threat of its use'. But in practice we are talking about the same thing.

Tilly's focus, however, is less on the event than on the process of alienation and regrouping that precedes it, and here his analyses are 'doggedly anti-Durkheimian, resolutely pro-Marxian, but sometimes indulgent to Weber and sometimes reliant on Mill' (Tilly 1978, p. 48). Instead of using the terms 'process' and 'event' he distinguishes between *revolutionary situations* and *revolutionary outcomes* and sees the revolutionary outcome as the product of the emergence of multiple sovereignty in what he terms a revolutionary situation. In doing so he correctly recognizes the fundamental point about revolution, that it is the product of a contest: whether the outcome is no change, a *coup*, a silent revolution or a great revolution depends on circumstances and the amount of power mobilized by the contenders. No view that seeks to explain revolution solely from the point of view of the government or solely from the point of view of the opposition will therefore be able to explain properly what is going on.

There are, he argues (Tilly 1978, p. 200), three causes for the emergence of multiple sovereignty: first, the appearance of contenders or coalitions of contenders advancing 'exclusive alternative claims' to power; second, a commitment to those claims by a substantial sector of the public; and third, the unwillingness or inability of the government forces to suppress the contenders or those who support their claims. For Tilly the importance of the first (as for the Marxists and for Moore) is the part that ideas play in advancing justification for the alternative claims, and hence the role of the intellectuals in this process. As regards the second, Tilly's views have much in common with those of Ted Gurr (1970), James C. Davies (1962) and Neil Smelser (1962), that it is in the field of attitudinal analyses that the propensity to revolution will be detected. As regards the third, the key question is what is the balance between government and opposition? Hence, while recognizing the crucial importance of the armed forces, and in the same connection, the after-effects of war, Tilly is inclined to place more emphasis on the effects of inefficiency than of conspiracy in reducing the efficacy of the defending forces.

Revolutionary outcomes, Tilly hence argues (Tilly 1978, pp. 211–12), depend on two things in addition to the presence of a revolutionary situation. These are: 'revolutionary coalitions between challengers and members of the polity'; and control of 'substantial' force by the revolutionary contenders and their allies. How much force, then, is 'substantial'? As Tilly has earlier noted, Ted Gurr (1970, pp. 235–6) hypothesizes that 'The likelihood of internal war increases as the ratio of dissident to regime coercive control approaches equality'. He does not comment on this claim, but as a statement about internal war (i.e. a revolutionary situation) it is quite likely not to be true, as internal, like external, wars are as likely to break out because of over-confidence on one side or the other, as for example in the Gulf War of 1980. What is needed for a revolutionary *outcome*, surely, is enough force to defeat the government. But no revolutionary who gives the risks of failure any thought is likely to make do with just enough force. So this quantity cannot be taken as a guide to how much force will actually be deployed.

The force actually used to achieve a revolutionary outcome, Tilly argues, will depend on whether revolution is seen as a 'tension-release' mechanism or as a 'contention' model. Each has its advocates, though both are in fact probably true: a revolutionary outcome is the product of contention and so there may be little or no violence in advance of the action itself, *but* the action itself is hazardous to the contenders, so they will be likely to seek to acquire overwhelming force capabilities if they are given the time to do so. Only if pre-empted by the government are they likely to go ahead with insufficient resources and trust to luck. Whatever happens, victory in a revolutionary situation will go to the side achieving the minimum necessary force (MNF) within the critical time (CT) for it to overcome the opposition. However the outcome in this limited sense (i.e. the event), does not exhaust the effects of force on the polity. Tilly correctly recognizes (with Gurr and others) that the greater the use of force the more probable far-reaching structural change becomes, and hypothesizes (though he does not carry this argument very far) that the greater the change that occurs in the first short stage of consolidation the more likely it is that the changes will be extensive and permanent – these are, he suggests, the 'great revolutions'. Like many other writers, however, he tends to support the widespread and incorrect assumption that the converse is the case, as shown by his comment that 'Military coups almost never produce any significant structural change . . . *because* they involve minor rearrangements among extremely limited sets of contenders' (Tilly, 1978, p. 220, emphasis added), despite the fact that, as he goes on to explain, where such a contender achieves power and makes an alliance with previously unrepresented social groups (Turkey, Japan), then far-reaching change is possible. He concludes by encouraging his fellow historians to build up detailed pictures of collective action which will form part in time of a wider collective analysis.

Tilly, therefore, accommodates the politics of violence to the process of interest-articulation and coalition-forming which is the well trodden field of the sociologist and political scientist, while recognizing the differences which the use of violence brings. If there is a criticism it is that emphasis on the practice of collective violence, for which Tilly accepts a 'brute harm' (Tilly 1978, p. 176) conception, over-emphasizes the sources of violence without perhaps going far enough to elucidate the way in which leadership translates the propensity to violence into effective collective action with a political outcome. Studies of collective violence known to him are those from the United States and Western Europe. The evidence from these is that the bulk of the killing and wounding is done by pro-government forces and it is the rule and not the exception for a riot both to begin and end with police violence. (Recent evidence from Latin America, we can add, confirms this view.) 'The chief source of variation in collective violence is the operation of the polity' (Tilly 1978, p. 182). If this is the case, we cannot escape the conclusion that collective violence is primarily a political phenomenon, and in so far as revolutions are the product of collective violence it is the political causes rather than the economic or social conditions that are decisive.

Philosophical explanations

Modern philosophical explanations of revolution are still dominated by the challenging and always provocative work of Hannah

Arendt. Arendt's *On Revolution* (1963) stemmed from a seminar on 'The United States and the Revolutionary Spirit' held at Princeton University in the spring of 1959, and is concerned in the first instance with the interrelationship of war and revolution; for to her wars and revolutions have been the chief feature of the twentieth century, and if, as she argues, both have outlived their ideological justifications, they have left a major question mark over the future.

For Arendt revolution is one of the most recent of political phenomena. But the metaphor of revolution takes us back to the most ancient traditions of politics and the uncomfortable fact that, according to these oldest of tales, politics has its origin in crime. Revolution is the search for freedom, and revolutionaries are those who fight for freedom in the face of tyranny. But in Europe the French Revolution, to Arendt, failed to achieve the objectives of its proponents, foundered in the Terror and yielded in turn to a dictatorship, while the American Revolution was able to accomplish the objectives of the men and women who had started it and establish a new order of the ages (*novus ordo saeculorum*) in the Western Hemisphere dedicated to 'the pursuit of happiness'. This was, to Arendt (1963, p. 135), an event of transcendental significance: 'not only the American Revolution but everything that happened before and after "was an event within an Atlantic civilization as a whole"'.

> We today are still under the spell of this historical development, and so we may find it difficult to understand that revolution on the one hand, and constitution and foundation on the other, are like correlative conjunctions.
>
> (Arendt 1963, p. 122)

Who, then, are the true revolutionaries? For Arendt, with revolution a quest for freedom, they are those that constitute Liberty and build a society within which it can be attained. But, as she observes, one of the odd consequences of the belief that freedom has been secured only for America is the sundering of the United States from the European revolutionary tradition. 'The point is unpleasantly driven home when even revolutionaries on the American continent speak and act as though they knew by heart the texts of revolutions in France, in Russia, and in China, but had never heard of such a thing as an American Revolution' (Arendt 1963, p. 218). Part of the reason, as Arendt warns her countryfolk, is America's 'own failure to remember that a revolution gave birth to the United States and that the republic was brought into existence by no "historical necessity" and no organic development, but by a deliberate act: the foundation of freedom' (Arendt 1963, p. 219), for this failure only serves to confirm to others that the French Revolution is the only true model for what they seek.

Now a French reader might reasonably argue that today the French Fifth Republic secures to its citizens the blessings of freedom every bit as much as the United States. Was not that quintessentially American emblem, the Statue of Liberty, moulded in France and presented to the sister republic across the ocean? Did the American Revolution not contain its own hidden flaw, which gaped open when in the name of the Constitution of 1787 the men of Virginia and South Carolina sought to exclude their black brethren from the blessings of freedom and a Civil War followed which was one of the most savage events even in a world history that has since seen the twentieth century? Might Latin Americans (for example) who saw the curious affinity of US governments for tinpot Latin American dictators get the impression, however wrong it might be, that talk of an American Revolution was merely a façade for a new and insidious imperialism? And was there in fact any connection between affluence and freedom, and, if so, what precisely was the nature of that connection? On this at any rate Arendt is both ready and forthright:

> When we were told that by freedom we understood free enterprise, we did very little to dispel this monstrous falsehood, and all too often we have acted as though we too believed it was wealth and abundance that were at stake in the postwar conflict between the 'revolutionary' countries in the East and the West. Wealth and economic well-being, we have asserted, are the fruits of freedom, while we should have been the first to know that this kind of 'happiness' was the blessing of this country prior to the Revolution, and that its cause was natural abundance under 'mild government,' and neither political freedom nor the unchained, unbridled 'private initiative' of capitalism, which in the absence of natural wealth has led everywhere to unhappiness and mass poverty.
>
> (Arendt 1963, p. 219)

And, she prophetically added: 'Economic growth may one day turn out to be a curse rather than a good, and under no conditions can it either lead into freedom or constitute a proof for its existence' (Arendt 1963, pp. 219–20).

Freedom, then, is a quite distinctive quality, a good in itself, which it is the highest achievement of human society to attain. The problem of revolution is that its spirit has failed to find appropriate institutions in which to express itself. The book therefore concludes with a clear statement of what the author takes to be the practical consequences of trying to realize this objective: not party government, which she regards as government by an elite chosen by the people, but self-government by deputies of 'elementary republics'.

Ironically, this is of course the very idea enshrined in the system of 'soviets' or committees which formed the basis for dual power in Russia, and which Lenin and his followers after the October Revolution were to subject to the will of the Party. No doubt this would not have happened, or at least would not have happened so quickly, had it not been for the inexperience of the Russian people in the virtues of free society. The price of liberty is eternal vigilance, and the lesson of American history is that there has to be a continual desire to reform and restructure institutions in the direction of greater freedom or in time that liberty will be lost. Almost all modern democratic societies are the product of revolution: Switzerland, The Netherlands, Britain, Sweden, the United States, France. But all of those societies have had to withstand challenges to their freedom and the only reason why they are still democratic is that their revolutions were partly successful and so the effects of the revolutionary settlement have yet to be fully eroded. Since Arendt wrote, in the United States Watergate and the Iran-Contra scandal have reminded us how little we can trust those we elect to do our will. Lying becomes 'a cover story', condoning breaches of the law is termed 'maintaining plausible deniability', bandits and thugs are hailed as 'freedom fighters', killing civilians is called 'striking at economic targets'. (Euphemism is not peculiar to liberal democracies: in China shooting down students is a 'great victory', and in killing them the Army is 'working for the people'.)

The democratic leader is, of course, in a difficult position. To lead is not simply to follow the unformed opinion of others, but to show them how the good they desire can be attained by acceptable means. People may have a clear idea of both the ends they seek and the means they wish to use, but the selected means do not in fact always lead to the chosen ends. It is the essence of democratic leadership to sense the underlying purpose and to establish a coalition in favour of implementing it in a way that is compatible with the spirit of the society. Unfortunately, democratic leaders do not always stop at this point. Driven by a terrible hunger for power and the adulation of the masses they become less and less responsible, branding all opposition to their will as sedition and ultimately, in a terrible perversion of liberty, using the very fact of opposition as evidence of the rightness of their ideas. Again and again in recent years rulers and elites have been revealed to the world with their fingers, metaphorically speaking, in the till of liberty, trying, often all too successfully, to steal the good will of their followers by controlling the information on which they have to make up their minds.

In fact the legacy of the Enlightenment is a dual one. Arendt focuses on the realization of Liberty. But Liberty is to be achieved, and is *only* to be achieved, by the exercise of Reason. To sacrifice either one to the other is to deny the potential as lessons for human advancement which distinguishes both the French and American Revolutions. Reason tells us that Liberty cannot be achieved by enthroning irrationality. Hence if governments are instituted to secure Liberty, they have to be rational governments and they have to be limited in their powers. Since 1945 the most chilling example of the ultimate consequences of believing in both the unrestrained power of government and in the need to eradicate the rational from a culture has been the killing fields of Cambodia in Year Zero, when independent teams of Pol Pot's Khmer Rouge peasant revolutionaries deliberately smashed every vestige of advanced civilization, depopulated the towns and killed anyone who looked like an intellectual, acting, they believed, on 'authority' – though on whose has never become clear.

The role of ideas

In leading us to reassess the role of ideas in political and social life, however, Arendt has rightly laid emphasis on the central paradox of revolution: revolution is both violence, the negation of political reason, and rebuilding, the epitome of rational social organization. However far and dim the objective of that process of rebuilding might be, it is extremely rare for any use of violence in politics not to be represented as a small step in the ultimate improvement of mankind. Even the promoters of the many *coups* that have so successfully held up the progress of the world since 1945 have had goals and objectives, among which we can be sure there figures some notion of an ideal society. It is probable that for them that society is one in which the *coup*-promoter stars as a wise ruler who gives orders which are unconditionally obeyed by clean, healthy, hard-working peasants who know their place in society and work willingly and long in the fields of the great estates so that all can be enriched and the wife of the leader can have her hair done in Paris. But, however spurious, however inappropriate, that idea exists and has real political outcomes in terms of commands and decree-laws that are enforced, if necessary, at the point of a gun. If, then, ideas are so powerful, why should not we, the people, reassert that we want our ideas to be heard?

Ideas are central to the notion of revolution, first because all political life is structured in terms of ideas, second because revolution, an essentially-contested concept, is a label attached to events or sequences of events which mean different things to different people, and third because the very concept of change, the yardstick which people use to determine whether or not a revolution has occurred, is itself culturally determined.

The recognition of the power of ideas is, of course, foremost among the reasons why revolution is alternatively admired and feared. Psychologically, it is highly disturbing to find that a profound change has taken place in the *Weltanschauung* generally held in the society of which one is a member. Erich Fromm (1960), indeed, argued that the freedom hailed as the chief virtue of politics by Arendt was something that many free-born citizens feared and were prepared to be rid of, if a suitable dictator came along who promised to take the burden of personal responsibility off their shoulders. And in the psychological concept of 'cognitive dissonance' we find the reason why people who have made far-reaching changes in their lifestyles can soon be found arguing that the new order of things is the most natural in the world.

If revolution is a mental construct, however, it is not one that is easily accepted. Ideas have always travelled freely across state boundaries and writers on revolution have long recognized the role of the foreign traveller in spreading new social ideas. To the conservative, therefore, revolution is easily seen as the outcome of successful propaganda or even as some kind of social contagion which spreads from society to society. There is something in this, but if revolution is a social contagion, the best remedy (on the medical analogy) is immunization, not surgery, for it is within society and not from abroad that the essential preconditions for revolution develop, and if those preconditions do not exist, they certainly cannot be introduced arbitrarily other than by the overwhelming use of force such as follows a military defeat.

No government can be overthrown that is genuinely stable. What constitutes genuine stability is, however, debatable as long as the question of what constitutes political stability has not been satisfactorily resolved. The main division in the literature is between those who regard stability as something which is either present or absent, and those who regard it as a continuum. But there are also substantial disagreements between various authorities on other aspects of the problem, giving rise to six main schools of thought in all. In consequence there is extensive confusion as to the causes and effects of political instability. A later project will be to explore further the way in which political regimes are displaced and the probability of this happening and so to clarify the vexed question of what constitutes a political risk.

For, as noted above, the greatest irony is that regardless of the uncertainty that surrounds the most basic concepts, practical politicians have not hesitated to engage in measures directed at the 'destabilization' of unfriendly regimes. By 'destabilization' is understood, for example, the measures taken by the Nixon–Kissinger team at the White House to exacerbate the financial crisis in Chile and in intriguing with the armed forces to dislodge President Allende. Setting aside the characteristic euphemism we are left, in effect, with a practical exercise in spreading the 'contagion' of revolution. Similar measures are reported to have been taken in the 1980s by the Reagan administration against the governments of Nicaragua and Grenada, in the latter case leading to the divisions in the regime that opened the way to US intervention. More recently, on the other side of the world, the Afghan government has denounced Western support for the Islamic fundamentalist Mujaheddin, while following the student unrest in Beijing the Chinese leadership has been complaining that students have been spreading the 'contagion' of counter-revolution.

The possibility of transplanting revolutionary (or counter-revolutionary) ideas between societies is, of course, the very reason why revolution is both hated and feared by incumbent governments and admired and emulated by those who seek to change the world and make it a better place. If it is a metaphor for change, it is the ultimate one, signifying to all alike power, efficacy and irresistibility. However, if it is a metaphor, the idea that it can be propagated is itself a myth. If it is not, there are still several good reasons for believing that the contagion theory of revolution can be discounted.

To begin with, it is clear from historical evidence that the main causes of the outbreak of revolution are peculiar to the societies in which they arise. What is surprising about the major instances, in fact, is the extent to which they are expected (both hoped for and feared) long in advance, but they depart from all the expectations that people had of them. Their initial outbreak is followed by strange happenings that are peculiar to the time and place. This may well be partly because governments are themselves alerted by the resemblance to known events to react sooner or more effectively than they otherwise would. It is also partly because of the nature of technological progress, which ensures that the balance of forces as between government and opposition is constantly changing.

Secondly, the main factor leading to the outbreak of revolution is the action of the government; it is the government that precipitates revolution. Governments that abstain from firing upon peaceful demonstrations, avoid outrages to sacred symbols, do not behave vindictively towards their political opponents, avoid bringing themselves into contempt by their greed, and avoid antagonizing the armed forces may weather storms that have wrecked many other governments before and since. But even bad and unpopular governments may retain power when the main challenge to their authority is seen to come from abroad.

Hence, thirdly, even if the message that comes from abroad is seductive, it does not follow that its impact in the new society will be the same. At the time of the French Revolution groups in The Netherlands, in Germany and in Italy did emulate the events in France to some extent. The majority of these events were of little significance, however, until the French armies arrived. The October Revolution of 1917 was imitated in the same fashion, but the risings in Budapest, Reval and Shanghai were suppressed, and until the Russian armies drove westward in 1945 the only other place to experience a Russian-style revolution was Outer Mongolia. Ideas, whether of revolution or of anything else, have to be interpreted within a social framework, and if that social framework is different (as it necessarily is) from the one in which the ideas originated, then their outcome will necessarily be different.

The fear of new ideas is, however, a commonplace of politics, for politicians gain much of their support from their ability to reassure their followers that they at least understand how the world really works. Any shift in the pattern spells trouble; a major shift may take the situation beyond the politician's abilities to control. Hence, for example, while major initiatives are being taken by President Gorbachev and the Soviet Union to end the state of division that has existed in Europe since 1947 (and which continues to threaten all our lives every minute of every day), and these initiatives are, however cautiously, being accepted in principle by the US administration, the British Prime Minister, Margaret Thatcher, has been speaking incongruously of the dangers of communism, the need to retain short-range nuclear weapons in Europe, and the threat to national sovereignty posed by the unlikely contingency of a socialist Brussels. But then she herself has, in her way, been trying to carry out revolutionary changes, and she would not be the first would-be revolutionary to find that the structures of society are intensely resistant to change from above, and that the very concept of a revolution from above is, in fact, a contradiction in terms.

Bibliography

Adelman, Jonathan R. (1985). *Revolution, Armies, and War: A Political History*. Boulder, Colo., Lynne Rienner.

Adorno, T. W., Frenkel Brunswik, Else, Levinson, Daniel J. and Sanford, R. Nevitt (1964). *The Authoritarian Personality*. New York, John Wiley.

Allison, Graham T. (1971). *Essence of Decision: Explaining the Cuban Missile Crisis*. Boston, Little, Brown.

Andriole, Stephen J. and Hopper, Gerald W. (1984). *Revolution and Political Stability*. London, Frances Pinter.

Arendt, Hannah (1963). *On Revolution*. London, Faber & Faber.

Birnbaum, Pierre (1988). *States and Collective Action: The European Experience*. Cambridge, Cambridge University Press.

Borkenau, Franz (1937). 'State and revolution in the Paris Commune, the Russian Revolution, and the Spanish Civil War', *Sociological Review*, 29, January, pp. 41–75.

Brier, Alan (1982). 'Revolution as a form of political succession', unpublished paper for Planning Session on Political Succession, ECPR Joint Sessions of Workshops, Freiburg.

Brier, Alan and Calvert, Peter (1975). 'Revolution in the 1960s', *Political Studies*, 32, no. 1, March, pp. 1–11.

Brinton, Crane (1952). *The Anatomy of Revolution*. New York, Vintage Books.

Butterfield, L. H. (1959). 'July 4 in 1826', *American Heritage*, 6, no. 4, p. 14.

Calvert, Peter (1967). 'Revolution, the politics of violence', *Political Studies*, 15, no. 1, February, pp. 1–11.

Calvert, Peter (1969). 'The dynamics of political change', *Political Studies*, 17, no. 4, pp. 446–57.

Calvert, Peter (1970a). *Revolution*. London, Pall Mall and Macmillan.

Calvert, Peter (1970b). *A Study of Revolution*. Oxford, Clarendon Press.

Calvert, Peter (1982). *The Concept of Class: An Historical Introduction*. London, Hutchinson.

Calvert, Peter (1984). *Revolution and International Politics*. London, Frances Pinter.

Chorley, Katharine C. (1943). *Armies and the Art of Revolution*. London, Faber & Faber.

Cohan, A. S. (1975). *Theories of Revolution: An Introduction*. London, Thomas Nelson & Sons.

Davies, James Chowning (1962). 'Toward a theory of revolution', *American Sociological Review*, 43, no. 1, February, p. 5.

Davies, James Chowning (ed.) (1971). *When Men Revolt and Why: A Reader in Political Violence and Revolution*. New York, The Free Press.

Debray, Régis (1965). 'Latin America: the Long March', *New Left Review*, 33, September–October, p. 17.

Djilas, Milovan (1957). *The New Class: An Analysis of the Communist System*. London, Thames & Hudson.

Dunn, John (1972). *Modern Revolutions: An Introduction to the Analysis of a Political Phenomenon*. Cambridge, Cambridge University Press.

Dunn, John (1985). 'Understanding revolutions' in John Dunn, *Rethinking Modern Political Theory: Essays 1979–83*. Cambridge, Cambridge University Press.

Dunn, John (1989). *Modern Revolutions: An Introduction to the Analysis of a Political Phenomenon*, 2nd edn. Cambridge, Cambridge University Press.

Eckstein, Harry, ed. (1964). *Internal War: Problems and Approaches*. New York, The Free Press.

Eckstein, Harry (1965). 'On the etiology of internal wars', *History and Theory*, 4, pp. 133–4.

Edwards, Lyford P. (1970). *The Natural History of Revolution*. Chicago, The University of Chicago Press.

Eisenstadt, S. N. (1978). *Revolution and the Transformation of Societies*. New York, The Free Press.

Ellwood, Charles A. (1905). 'A psychological theory of revolutions', *American Journal of Sociology*, 11, pp. 49–59.

Elster, Jon (1983). *Sour Grapes: Studies in the Subversion of Rationality*. Cambridge, Cambridge University Press.

Finer, S. E. (1976). *The Man on Horseback: The Role of the Military in Politics*. 2nd revised edn. Harmondsworth, Penguin Books.

France, Anatole (1930). *Penguin Island*. Crown 8vo Edition, London, The Bodley Head.

Fromm, Erich (1960). *The Fear of Freedom*. London, Routledge & Kegan Paul.

Gallie, W. B. (1955–6). 'Essentially-contested concepts', *Proceedings of the Aristotelian Society*, 56, pp. 167–98.

Gamson, William A. (1975). *The Strategy of Social Protest*. Homewood, Ill., The Dorsey Press.

Giddens, Anthony (1989). *Sociology*. Oxford, Polity Press.

Goldstone, J. (1982). 'The comparative and historical study of revolutions', *Annual Review of Sociology*, 8.

Goodspeed, D. J. (1962). *The Conspirators: A Study of the Coup d'Etat*. London, Macmillan.

Guevara, Ernesto Che (1967). *Guerrilla Warfare*. New York and London, Monthly Review Press.

Gurr, Ted Robert (1970). *Why Men Rebel*. Princeton, NJ, Princeton University Press.

Hall, John A. (1985). *Powers and Liberties: The Causes and Consequences of the Rise of the West*. Harmondsworth, Penguin.

Hardin, Russell (1982). *Collective Action*. Baltimore, Md., Johns Hopkins University Press for Resources for the Future.

Jackson, Geoffrey (1973). *People's Prison*. London, Faber & Faber.

Janis, Irving L. (1972). *Victims of Groupthink: A Psychological Study of Foreign Policy Decisions and Fiascos*. Boston, Houghton Mifflin.

Johnson, Chalmers (1964). *Revolution and the Social System*. Stanford, Cal., The Hoover Institution on War, Revolution, and Peace, Stanford University.

Johnson, Chalmers (1966). *Revolutionary Change*. Boston, Little Brown.

Kuhn, Thomas S. (1970). *The Structure of Scientific Revolutions*, 2nd edn., Chicago, University of Chicago Press.

Kumar, Krishnan (1971). *Revolution: The Theory and Practice of a European Idea*. London, Weidenfeld & Nicolson.

Laurie, Peter (1970). *Beneath the City Streets: A Private Enquiry into the Nuclear Preoccupations of Government*. London, Allen Lane.

Le Bon, Gustave (1960). *The Crowd: A Study of the Popular Mind*, intro. Robert K. Merton. New York, Viking Press.

Leiden, Carl and Schmitt, Karl M. (1968). *The Politics of Violence: Revolution in the Modern World*. Englewood Cliffs, NJ, Prentice Hall.

Lenin, Vladimir Il'ych (1968). *State and Revolution*. New York, International Publishers.

MacIntyre, Alasdair (1973). 'Ideology, Social Science and Revolution', *Comparative Politics*, 5, no. 3, April, pp. 321–42.

MacIntyre, Alisdair (1983). 'Is a science of comparative politics possible?' in A. MacIntyre, ed., *Against the Self-images of the Age: Essays on Ideology and Philosophy*, 2nd edn. London, Duckworth.

Mann, Michael (1986). *The Sources of Social Power. Vol. I: A History of Power from the Beginning to 1760*. Cambridge, Cambridge University Press.

Martin, Everett Dean (1920). *The Behaviour of Crowds: A Psychological Study*. New York and London, Putnam.

Marx, Karl and Engels, Frederick (1962). *Selected Works*. Moscow, Foreign Languages Publishing House.

Mazlish, Bruce, Kaledin, Arthur D. and Ralston, David B., eds (1971). *Revolution: A Reader*. New York, Macmillan.

Migdal, Joel S. (1974). *Peasants, Politics and Revolution: Pressures toward Political and Social Change in the Third World*. Princeton, NJ, Princeton University Press.

Moore, Barrington, Jr (1969). *Social Origins of Dictatorship and Democracy: Lord and Peasant in the Making of the Modern World*. Harmondsworth, Penguin Books.

Moore, Barrington, Jr (1972). *Reflections on the Causes of Human Misery*. London, Allen Lane.

Mouzelis, Nicos P. (1986). *Politics in the Semi-Periphery: Early Parliamentarism and Late Industrialisation in the Balkans and Latin America*. Basingstoke, Macmillan.

Neumann, Sigmund (1949). 'The International Civil War', *World Politics*, 1, no. 3, April, pp. 333–50.

Olson, Mancur (1965). *The Logic of Collective Action*. Cambridge, Mass., Harvard University Press.

O'Kane, Rosemary H. T. (1987). *The Likelihood of Coups*. Aldershot, Gower.

O'Sullivan, Noel, ed. (1983). *Revolutionary Theory and Political Reality*. Brighton, Wheatsheaf.

Palmer, Robert R. (1959). *The Age of the Democratic Revolution*. Princeton, NJ, Princeton University Press.

Pettee, George Sawyer (1938). *The Process of Revolution*. New York, Harper and Brothers.

Popper, Karl Raimund (1962). *The Open Society and its Enemies*. 4th edn (revised), London, Routledge & Kegan Paul.

Popper, Karl Raimund (1957). *The Poverty of Historicism*. London, Routledge & Kegan Paul.

Porter, Roy and Teich, M., eds (1986). *Revolution in History*. Cambridge, Cambridge University Press.

Poulantzas, Nicos (1975). *The Crisis of the Dictatorships: Portugal, Greece, Spain*, trs. David Fernbach. London, New Left Books.

Rejaj, Mostafa (1977). *The Comparative Study of Revolutionary Strategy*. New York, David McKay.

Robertson, David (1985). *The Penguin Dictionary of Politics*. Harmondsworth, Penguin Books.

Roemer, John E. (1985). 'Rationalizing revolutionary ideology', *Econometrika*, 53, January, pp. 84–108.

Sartori, G. (1970). 'Concept misformation in comparative politics', *American Political Science Review*, 54.

Shafer, D. Michael (1988). *Deadly Paradigms: The Failure of U.S. Counterinsurgency Policy*. Princeton, NJ, Princeton University Press.

Skocpol, Theda (1979). *States and Social Revolutions: A Comparative Analysis of France, Russia and China*. Cambridge, Cambridge University Press.

Skocpol, Theda (1982). 'What makes peasants revolutionary?', *Comparative Politics*, 14, April, pp. 351–75.

Skocpol, Theda (1988). 'Social Revolutions and Mass Military Mobilization', *World Politics*, 40, no. 2, January, pp. 147–68.

Smelser, Neil J. (1962). *Theory of Collective Behaviour*. London, Routledge & Kegan Paul.

Smith, Dennis (1983). *Barrington Moore: Violence, Morality and Political Change*. London, Macmillan.

Sorokin, Pitrim Aleksandovitch (1925). *The Sociology of Revolution*. Philadelphia, Lippincott.

Spengler, Oswald (1923). *Der Untergang des Abendlandes: Umrissi einer Morphologie der Weltgeschichte*. Munich, Beck, 2 vols.

Taylor, Michael (1976). *Anarchy and Cooperation*. London, Wiley.

Taylor, Michael (1982). *Community, Anarchy and Liberty*. Cambridge, Cambridge University Press.

Taylor, Michael, ed. (1988). *Rationality and Revolution*. Cambridge, Cambridge University Press.

Therborn, Göran (1980). *What Does the Ruling Class Do When It Rules?* London, Verso.

Tilly, Charles (1975a). 'Revolutions and collective violence' in Fred I. Greenstein and Nelson W. Polsby, eds, *Handbook of Political Science*, III. Reading, Mass., Addison-Wesley, pp. 483–555.

Tilly, Charles, ed. (1975b). *The Formation of National States in Western Europe*. Princeton, NJ, Princeton University Press.

Tilly, Charles (1978). *From Mobilization to Revolution*. Reading, Mass., Addison-Wesley.

Tocqueville, Alexis de (1966). *The Ancien Régime and the French Revolution*, intro. Hugh Brogan, trs. Stuart Gilbert. London, Collins/Fontana.

Touraine, Alain (1977). *The Self-Production of Society*. Chicago, University of Chicago Press.

Touraine, Alain (1981). *The Voice and the Eye: An Analysis of Social Movements*. Cambridge, Cambridge University Press.

Toynbee, Arnold J. (1946). *A Study of History*. London, Oxford University Press for Royal Institute of International Affairs.

Trimberger, Ellen Kay (1972). 'A theory of elite revolutions', *Studies in Comparative International Development*, 7, no. 3, Fall, pp. 191–207.

Trimberger, Ellen Kay (1978). *Revolution from Above: Military Bureaucrats and Development in Japan, Turkey, Egypt and Peru*. New Brunswick, NJ, Transaction Books.

Trotter, William Finlayson (1953). *Instincts of the Herd in Peace and War*. London, Oxford University Press.

Wallerstein, Immanuel (1974a). *The Modern World-System: Capitalist Agriculture and the Origins of the European World-Economy in the Sixteenth Century*. New York, The Academic Press.

Wallerstein, Immanuel (1974b). 'The Rise and Future Demise of the World Capitalist System: Concepts for Comparative Analysis', *Comparative Studies in Society and History*, 16, no. 4, September, pp. 387–415.

Wilkinson, David (1975). *Revolutionary Civil War, the Elements of Victory and Defeat*. Palo Alto, Cal., Page-Ficklin Publications.

Winch, Peter (1958). *The Idea of a Social Science and its Relation to Philosophy*. London, Routledge.

Wolf, Eric (1970). *Peasant Wars of the Twentieth Century*. New York, Harper & Row.

Wolfenstein, E. Victor (1967). *The Revolutionary Personality: Lenin, Trotsky, Gandhi*. Princeton, NJ, Princeton University Press.

Zagorin, Perez (1982). *Rebels and Rulers, 1500–1600*. Cambridge, Cambridge University Press, 2 vols.

Zeitlin, Maurice (1988). *The Civil Wars in Chile (Or The Bourgeois Revolutions that Never Were)*. Princeton, NJ, Princeton University Press.

Index